Made for This

Hannah Garcia

New York | Los Angeles | London | Sydney

ISBN Hardcover: 978-1-952884-60-3

ISBN Softcover: 978-1-952884-03-0

Dedication

For all the women, young and older, who are in search of who they used to be, or seeking who they wish to become.

Table of Contents

CHAPTER 1

Family Ties

I remember standing at the door as a child waiting for my biological father to come pick me up for his court-ordered visits for the weekend. I remember keeping an eye out for his truck to pull in the driveway. More times than not, the phone would ring, and he would be calling to cancel, claiming whatever excuse he had. Or even worse, he just wouldn't show up at all. No call to cancel, no truck to pick me up. At times, I remember my mom telling me, on his behalf, that he said he had to work and that's why he couldn't get me for the weekend.

As time went on, I was hurt more and more by his absence and conversely encouraged by the presence of my stepfather's 's fearless love for me and my mother.

He not only gave us the gift of feeling complete as a family, he gifted me a brother.

I asked to be legally adopted and become a "Mason". When we were finalizing the adoption, the courts gave my biological father an ultimatum: pay the thousands he owed in back child support, serve a specific amount of time in jail, or relinquish his paternal rights and sign his shared custody over to my mom and stepdad. He signed me over. Without pause. I guess jail and paying what he owed wasn't worth it to have the right to be in my life. His freedom and money meant more to him than his own daughter.

For the remainder of my childhood and a large portion of my adulthood, I walked through life feeling not good enough. I mean, if my own father didn't want me, who would? Sure, I had a stepdad who had taken me on and loved me as his own. But there's a feeling of abandonment that comes with the feeling of not being worth the sacrifice to someone you thought loved you.

My biological father only loved me when it was convenient. When I was the cute kid to bring to family Christmas gatherings or show off to his girlfriend a as he played the part of 'doting father'. I had grown close to his family. I enjoyed playing with my cousins and seeing my grandmother, aunts, and uncles. I wanted to spend that time with them, because I loved them.

When I approached my mom about being adopted around age 11, she told me what I would be giving up. She warned me that I wouldn't be seeing his side of the family anymore until I was of legal age to make that decision to be a part of their lives outside of the courts.   It wasn't an easy decision to make.   What was even harder was having my heart broken every other weekend waiting on him to not show up.

I missed out on a lot of events with my cousins and the rest of his family when his parental rights were relinquished. I missed birthdays, weddings, funerals, graduation parties, and our weekend hoorahs. I missed it all. I never wanted them cut out of my life, but I knew I didn't want him in it either. Sometimes, we must give up something in order to gain something else. Sometimes, the hurt we are in isn't worth suffering anymore, and it seems like the better thing to do is just to remove it all together. Since then, I've be graced with not only being able to be a part of my cousins and other extended family's lives and having the hard conversation of reconciliation with my birth father. It was hard, but a good hard. It was a gift of forgiveness and an act of letting go that I needed to partake in, in order to move forward in my life. You can forgive someone for the wrong they've done to you without giving them a place in your life. Forgiveness is more about allowing yourself the gift of better-ness and letting go of bitterness.

Years of counseling and therapy helped me walk in that season of hard, but it didn't give me   everything I needed. Permission to love myself, despite the feeling of not good enough. Permission to not chase love in a negative way from other men. That didn't come until much later in my life. And it came at the expense of my dignity at times.

Hindsight is 20/20.

When I was looking to be loved, I was looking in all the wrong places. I was looking at what the world was dictating as truth and not what I grew up in church believing. Leaning in to the former - one of the ways I chased love was by hopping in to bed with a guy as soon as we entered a relationship. No rule dictated how long to wait. I needed and longed to feel love from a man, and that was the means in which I sought it.

Yes, my stepdad loved me and took me on as his own, even though our DNA wasn't the same. Yes, I knew that he would do anything for me. But that didn't cancel out the rejection I felt from the man who was supposed to play that role, yet continued to choose alcohol, his girlfriend, and whatever else tickled his fancy over his daughter. At the time, I didn't understand that the person I needed love from was myself.

Giving pieces of myself away to whomever would take them, stripped away at the value I placed on myself. My self-worth diminished with every piece of myself I gave away. Piece by piece, I lost myself. With every harsh word, opinion, and judgement aimed at me, I defined my existence. I allowed what people said - how they perceived me, my actions, and the ways I chose to perceive it - to be the definition of who I was. The negative ways of chasing my need to feel seen and be loved enabled me to spiral into a depression and exemplify behaviors that were impulsive and characteristic of someone with bipolar.

Later, in a counseling session at the age of 19, the diagnosis came. Bipolar with abandonment issues. It doesn't take a therapist to understand why I struggled with feeling rejected. Instead of seeking my Heavenly Father for love and acceptance, I sought what the world had to offer in those moments, and time and time again, I ended up hurt, sad, rejected, and lost. The prophet Jeremiah is known for his words of promise from God that there are plans for our future. Plans of goodness and hope. The tricky part comes when we don't exercise the latter. The part in verse 13 and 14 that says we must seek Him and that when we do seek Him, we find Him. Jeremiah 29:13 (King James Version) "And ye shall seek Me, and find Me, when ye search for Me with all your heart." We also find restoration and deliverance from the places in our lives that have held us captive. If I had leaned into that truth— the truth I grew up believing in Sunday school— I would have learned much sooner that hardships are tests of our faith. To see how we respond to the trials God puts in our lives and whether we choose to get back up when we fall, or stay down and become a victim. The thing is, we already have what it takes. We were given the gift of free will by God when He created us. We have the choice to persevere just as much as we have the choice of being the victim and staying down. Do we get back up like the Cardi B song instructs us, do we identify with what Kelly Clarkson says about what doesn't kill us makes us stronger, or do we choose to stay stagnant and be the 'wronged one' in a country song?

We have a choice, and we need to choose wisely.

Things that helped me:

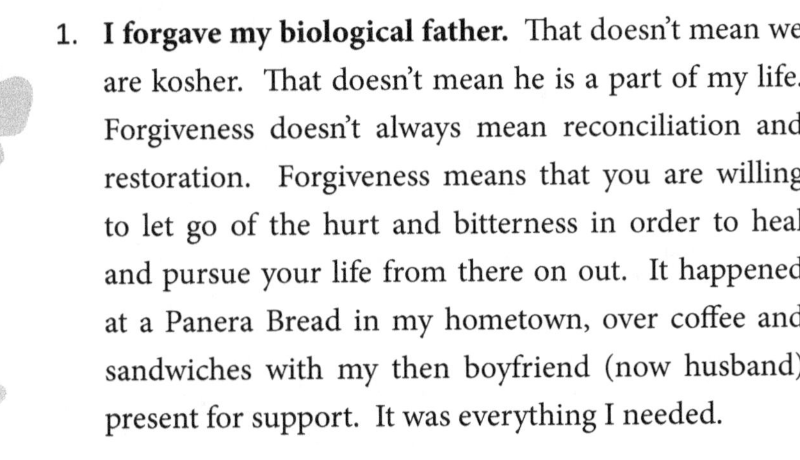

1. **I forgave my biological father.** That doesn't mean we are kosher. That doesn't mean he is a part of my life. Forgiveness doesn't always mean reconciliation and restoration. Forgiveness means that you are willing to let go of the hurt and bitterness in order to heal and pursue your life from there on out. It happened at a Panera Bread in my hometown, over coffee and sandwiches with my then boyfriend (now husband) present for support. It was everything I needed.

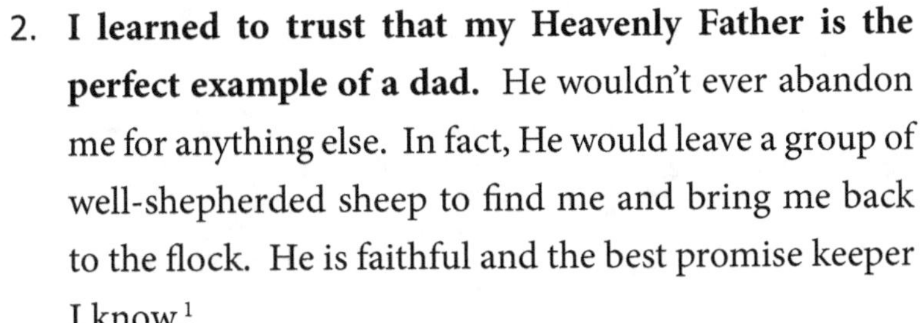

2. **I learned to trust that my Heavenly Father is the perfect example of a dad.** He wouldn't ever abandon me for anything else. In fact, He would leave a group of well-shepherded sheep to find me and bring me back to the flock. He is faithful and the best promise keeper I know.[1]

CHAPTER 2

Not Everything Happens for a Reason

Two weeks after I gave my life to Christ at the ripe age of 20, I was sexually assaulted by my ex-boyfriend. Talk about having your faith jilted.

We had just broken up shortly before, and I had gone over to his apartment to clear the air and have what I had hoped to be an adult conversation to come to an understanding, so as not to leave things on bad terms. He lived in the same town as me, after all.

After refusing to get back together with him and exchanging words, I said goodbye and was heading towards the front door. He grabbed me from behind and forced me to the ground. Some parts are blurry. I don't remember every detail, because I believe my brain kicked in to defense-mode to shield me from even more trauma. I do remember trying to escape. I remember being in between the couch and the coffee table feeling trapped on both sides, as well as being physically pinned down with his hands on my wrists. I do remember screaming 'no' and putting up a fight. I also remember not being able to get away, to the point where I gave up the fight to avoid any further injury.

When the assault was over, I ran as fast as I could to my car and drove home. The whole way home, not only was I questioning the point of being a Christian, I was also questioning things like: where was God? Why did He allow this to happen after I *just* committed my life to Him? If everything happens for a "reason" – what was the reason?

I still lived with my parents at the time, and I was nervous about having to talk to my mom. Fortunately, she had company, and they were in conversation when I got home. I headed upstairs and showered. I wanted to wash it all away, but there is no such thing as clean enough when you feel that level of dirty. There is no such thing as water hot enough or soap that makes enough suds to wash away the shame, embarrassment, and self-guilt that comes after being raped.

I was living with trauma. I felt numb and empty, like a robot going through the motions of life. A close friend invited me to a movie fest with some other friends at her house. Desperate to feel something again, I accepted the invite. The first flick – *Cold Mountain*. If you have seen the movie, you'll know the part I'm going to reference. There is a part where Natalie Portman is raped by one of the soldiers after giving away some of her animals. The scene was so triggering that I left the room and hid in the kitchen and cried. My friend came in to check on me, and I broke. I told her what happened, and she was so comforting and caring. She hugged me, and we prayed.

She was the only person who knew what had taken place. I was so afraid of not being believed, of being mocked and judged, that I carried it alone until I couldn't stand anymore.

I naively believed that everything happens for a reason. But that's just not true. God didn't allow me to be raped for a reason. I believed everything happened for a reason until I went through something so traumatic that there was no reason to be found. Folks would tell me that there is a reason. "Well, Janice, no, there isn't." There isn't a reason for the hard, crappy things in life, but there certainly is purpose and meaning to be found. Those words ring so hollow to someone who is in the midst of trauma and pain. We don't often understand or want to even try to understand how there is a "reason". Only when our minds are stilled, and our emotions find some level of calm are we able to begin reasoning with ourselves in a way to process.

A big realization happened two weeks later in the prayer room of my church. A friend of mine had been sexually assaulted a few days prior and was looking for help within the loving arms of our church family in Hilliard. The realization was monumental: I wasn't alone in my pain. I wasn't the only Christian who went through bad things, and I had people around me who were willing and able to carry the burden with me and walk alongside me. The simple knowledge I didn't have to go it alone, meant everything to me amid pain, shame, and loneliness. Even though a friend knew, I still felt alone and embarrassed. Meaning had been found.

Purpose wouldn't be found until many years later.

Jesus' brother James writes that "when troubles of any kind come your way, consider it an opportunity for great joy. For you know that when your faith is tested, your endurance has a chance to grow."[1] When the hard things come our way, God is allowing them as a test of our faith and how we respond to it. Are we going to lean into His guidance and seek His wisdom? Or are we going to throw our hands in the air and give up? That's where spiritual maturity is formed. In how we respond to God testing our faith when the trials show up.

I can sit here now and find gratitude in my assault. I can find purpose and meaning in the trauma. Mostly because I made way for Christ to do an incredible healing work within me. It took years to overcome the trauma. Years to learn how to stop self-medicating and hiding. I had to take on a survivor mentality and not a victim one. I had to understand that people who lacked an ability to show love and respect for their neighbor aren't a reflection of God. They are a reflection of the brokenness of the world we live in. I had to understand that even though God didn't allow me to be raped for a reason, He made way for me to find purpose in my life after. Sometimes, our mess becomes a message for someone else. Sometimes, proving to ourselves that we can overcome any trial, is the encouragement others need to know that they can do it, too. That right there is the meaning, the purpose.

Sometimes, life is the best teacher, and hindsight is always 20/20.

Life can be a great teacher if you live long enough to learn how to live it.

Tony Bennett said that in a documentary on Amy Winehouse, and it struck such a chord with me.

It's so true.

God uses circumstances in life to teach us how we need to be living it. Whether we need to slow down or seek Him more authentically. How to show up in situations as who we are called to be. Providing the catalyst for change that we need to pursue a better, more abundant life.

We don't always see the forest for the trees until we are out of the woods.

Like a Taylor Swift song, "some are built to fall apart, so we can fall together."

Things that helped me:

I forgave my rapist. Forgiveness isn't for the other person. It's for you. There are a few things about forgiveness that help us understand why it's so important to do. For starters, and most importantly, the Word of God says in Ephesians to forgive one another as Christ forgave you.[2]

Joyce Meyer articulates it well by saying that "harboring unforgiveness is like drinking poison and hoping your enemy will die." It is capital 'T' truth. Living in unforgiveness only makes you lean into bitterness. That does not serve you, nor does it serve your future self. Forgive. Seventy times seven. [3]

I was willing to lean into and own my trauma, so that I could be healed. Time is not your healer. Jesus is. The more I allowed myself to feel the hurt, to open my wounds, and pray for understanding of that event, the more I was enabled to gain perspective. I had to talk about it, pray about it, relive it, and cry about it for the healing to start to take place. Why? So that I could truly get some perspective and own my struggle. So that I could stop living as a victim and become a survivor. There is power in owning your struggle. There is victory in overcoming your trauma.

I accepted that it was not my fault. Nothing about what happened that day was my fault. Some people do not value others. Period. That is not my fault. Wanting to be a kind person and not have animosity between me and another human did not give him the right or permission. It also does not make it my fault. There was nothing different that I could have done to change the outcome of that day. What happened, happened. And trying to place blame on myself does not serve me or my healing.

CHAPTER 3

Members Only is not My Kind of Club

This one time, at band camp…. ha. Just kidding. I was never in band. I was barely good enough at playing the recorder in middle school to attempt to tryout. But I *loved* volleyball. In junior high, I had the privilege of playing volleyball for my school. I also got to play with a few of my good friends, as well. Afterschool practice was always so much fun. I loved all the things about it. *Bump, bump, bump it up. Set, set, set it high. Spike, spike, spike it hard. Rotate. Rotate.* Anyone else remember that little chant? One day, during practice in the gymnasium, I remember having this awful feeling in my stomach. I had no idea what it was. It was not too painful, but it was uncomfortable. And it was not exactly in my stomach. When practice was over, we headed to the locker room to get our stuff, and eventually join our parents in the carpool lane. I went to the bathroom first, pulled down my pants, and there was blood everywhere. All over my underwear and the back of my shorts. Was it visible to the other girls during practice? Probably. Did I have a change of clothes with me? Only pants, no underwear. In order to get out of the embarrassment as quickly as possible, I tied my sweatshirt around my waist and headed on out. Once I got in the car, I told my mom about it. In her sweet, sympathetic voice, she said, "Oh, Hannah, you started your period." Yuck. I had no idea what that meant other than, I was "becoming a woman". Let us pause for a slight chuckle at my expense.

We had just bought training bras a few weeks prior. Now, we had to make a trip to the feminine hygiene aisle at the store. Oh, what fun that was. Ha. Just kidding. Complete embarrassment aside, I was making a triumphant entry into puberty. And I wasn't exactly excited about it.

Like so many other girls, that wasn't the only time that *that time of the month* came without notice in school. All the way through high school, there were a handful of times each year that Aunt Flo came to visit without a heads up in the cramp department. Most of the time, I was prepared with the essentials on hand, to avoid another *blood on the back of my pants* debacle. A few times, however, due to forgetfulness to restock my essentials, I'd have to ask the dreaded question to female classmates, "Do you have a pad or a tampon I can use?" Oh, what fun.

If you ever saw a girl walking a certain distance ahead of her friends and they were checking out her butt in the hall, it's because they were checking to see if the gift Aunt Flo brought with her had left a mark on her pants. They had her back, by checking out her backside in a quick, nonchalant way. It's a girl thing. Like when we go to the bathroom together in bars. I would potentially be breaking Girl Code if I went into details on that one, so we will leave the reference as is.

What strikes me as funny about all the things girls do to have each other's backs, is that there a million more that happen that do nothing but tear each other down. Like making your *friend* the topic of conversation when she leaves the table. Or when another friend enters the picture and *threatens* your current best friendship, there is only half-ass inclusion. Behind their backs, there is story-telling that's inaccurate, or only being in the friendship for some gain, like access to their pool membership, or to have somewhere to go that has a computer to burn CDs off Napster. Half-ass inclusion. Because it is threatening to the little pink bubble that we've been living in that has a *members only* rule. You can come to club outings, but club meetings are off limits.

One of the things that always troubled me in various stages of my life, was how hard it was to find true friends. Often, I was used for what materialistic things I had brought to a friendship. How I could help when things got hard, whether it was financially or providing a safe space for a weekend. How I was there as someone's sound board in private, but no claim to friendship in the public eye or on social media. What hurt the most was when friendships would come to an end because they valued sugar-coated lies over the truth. Like our friendship was disposable, had an expiration date, or terms and conditions I did not know about. I was never the friend to lie or sugar-coat things. I was never the friend to talk crap behind your back. I was the one that said the hard things to your face and defended your honor behind your back. Even when other friends would make a member of the group's failing marriage the topic of conversation at a church luncheon. Some would attribute these things to small town life and gossip and plain old "how it is". I attribute it to people who are not the friends they seem on the outside.

It's taken me until my mid-30s to find some solid friends who are exactly my kind of people. And the kind of people who would call me their kind of people. The kind who tell me the truth, encourage me, do not talk smack behind my back, and always serve up respect at the lunch table. The kind who let me sit with them at club meetings and club outings, while also including everyone else to come sit with us, as well. The kind of friends who push me to be the best me I can be, while simultaneously holding me accountable. Years of tears and lost "friendships" have reaped the best rewards. A tribe to call my own.

Sometimes, we must learn the kind of friends we do not want, the ones we don't need, and the type we want to be to show us who our people are. It is not always like it is in television shows and movies. Sometimes, it is rather serendipitous. Sometimes, you are looking to learn how to go it alone, with only your faith and your family to lean on, and God shows you your village while you're on the journey.

Jim Henson, creator of the Muppets, has a great quote that fits perfectly. "There isn't a word yet for old friends who have just met." They need to find one, because I cannot find the right ones myself, only feelings – very beautiful ones. On second thought, maybe that is better than words. Those feelings are followed by a few joyous tears, because it's taken so long to get here. And shedding every dead weight friend along the way has been worth it.

Some people are not your people. Some people are not for you. And that is okay. There may be some tears shed, and some feelings hurt when you lose a friend, especially one you thought would be forever. It hurts like a breakup with the guy you thought you would one day marry. The cut can be that deep. And when you reflect on the loss, it will hurt. It will feel like salt in a wound. You can place blame on how you could have worded that harsh truth a little nicer without compromising the truth, itself. You can wonder if they think of you and miss you the way you still do at times. Or wonder if you make it into their thoughts and prayers. Truth is you will never know, and it is not worth asking. The answer will never be what you want. Leave Pandora's Box alone. It is closed for a reason. Pray for them, pray for yourself and your own healing, and move on. And like a CeeLo Green song, "although there's pain in your chest, still wish them the best."

It's not worth the price of admission to stay in a club that only allows you to be a part-time member, that makes your name the topic of conversation when you go to the bathroom or can't make it to the church luncheon. If anything costs you your self-worth, dignity, or causes you to have anxiety about what's happening in your absence, it's too expensive. Concerns for a friend in their absence disguised as prayer request is still gossip, and like Sweet Brown said, "Ain't nobody got time for that."

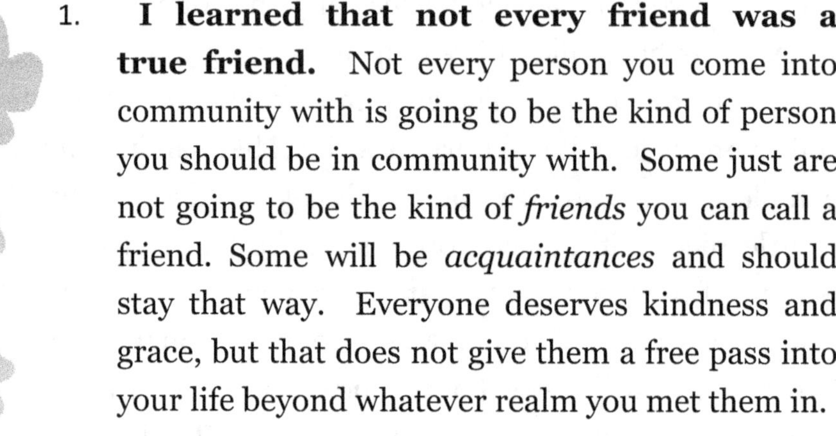

1. **I learned that not every friend was a true friend.** Not every person you come into community with is going to be the kind of person you should be in community with. Some just are not going to be the kind of *friends* you can call a friend. Some will be *acquaintances* and should stay that way. Everyone deserves kindness and grace, but that does not give them a free pass into your life beyond whatever realm you met them in.

2. **I had to forgive myself of wrongdoing, whether they chose to forgive me or not.** And I had to forgive them for hurting me. That does not always bring forth instant healing, but it brings forth enough closure to be able to move on. Not every friendship that has a falling out is going to be reconciled. Not every relationship is worth reconciling. Some people just are not for you, and you're not for them. And there is nothing wrong with that.

3. **I recommend not trashing them or the picture memories you have.** I used to delete pictures off social media or throw mementos in the trash because I was hurting. Don't. It may seem like a good idea at the time to get them out of sight and remove all memory of that relationship. But one day, you may want to look back and reminisce or have them if the friendship ends up being

restored. Put them in a box and hide it in your closet. Move the pictures from your camera or social media to a file on your computer or a private album on your device. You can then decide, after you have healed from the hurt much later, if you want all memory gone with the wind. Learn from my mistakes.

CHAPTER 4

Truth Hurts

I did not start dating until after I was out of high school. High school was not the greatest for me. I was not the popular, pretty girl I wanted to be. I felt like an outcast and went through most of it unseen and unnoticed. I had a handful of friends who I felt were good friends, until one of them made copies of a letter I had written her and distributed it throughout the school. I was the talk of my small-town high school for about a week or two. The crappy part was that the details of that letter were a lie. I was good at making up stories of imaginary boyfriends from other schools, so that I could feel seen and get in with the cool kids. I had a need to feel significant, even if it meant I was also a liar. I had such a desperate need to get attention, be popular, and be noticed by the cute boys, that I was willing to compromise my integrity. To answer your internal question, no Pam, the boyfriend from Lakewood never existed. I just had a need to fit in and feel like I was a part of the group.

It turns out, there are six basic human needs, according to Tony Robbins. Some are for personality and achievement sake, while the others are spiritual needs. There are six in total, and we are all composed of two of them. One from the personal, and one from the spiritual. The six basic human needs are: certainty, variety, significance, love and connection, and growth and contribution.

The first four of the six are the personal, and the last two are spiritual.

The first four can work in paradox to each other. Meaning that certainty and variety can become imbalanced, leaving one to crave excitement and adventure in an otherwise predictable kind of lifestyle. The same goes with significance vs. love and connection. Significance shows up as the need to have meaning, feel special, pride, feeling needed or wanted, having a sense of importance, and feeling worthy of love. And if you spend too much time gaining significance, you may have trouble finding deep intimate relationships that thrive on love and connection.[1]

It does not take a rocket scientist to figure out why it was hard to keep friends as a child and that I needed to feel popular in high school. They are paradoxes on the core *human needs* spectrum. Too much imbalance paved the way for the scale to tip. No wonder I was bipolar.

Later in life when I was entering into my young adulthood, I started to feel such a conviction from the Holy Spirit about all the lying I had done, that I eradicated my lies and started always telling the truth. Bluntly. I wanted to be "known" as brutally honest. Really leaning on the brutal side at times. I traded one bad habit for another. The white lies and stories of things that had checked all the boxes for what it took to be in the "in crowd" were replaced with cold hard truths of whatever I felt that person needed to hear. The scale tipped. Possibly even flopped on its head.

Some of these *hard truths* that I felt "they *should* hear" were the exact things that would destroy a friendship or make things awkward at work with a colleague. There are old phrases that contradict each other when it comes to honesty. Our parents used to tell us the same thing Thumper shared in Disney's *Bambi*. "If you can't say anything nice, don't say anything at all." The other is on the opposite end, justifying the need for brutal honesty in a world that thirsts for authenticity and vulnerability, "forget 'if you can't say anything nice, don't say anything at all', people need to hear the truth." Here is the thing that I have learned about being brutally honest: it's just brutal. There is a way to speak the truth and speak it in kindness and love. Not that it will necessarily be received in love, but at least it's spoken with the attempt to be kind without sacrificing the need to be honest. There is a phrase that I do think is relevant to whichever side of the spectrum you find yourself on when it comes to being brutally honest. That, "truth will sound like hate to those that hate the truth." Some folks want to stay in their situation simply out of stubbornness. Some have an extreme paralysis in being too closed-minded to see that new information can bring forth a different perspective, opinion, and approach. Others have a commitment to simply misunderstanding you, and whatever you do or say. When you start to learn and evolve into who you are created to be, your growth will be involuntarily perceived as an attack on others who are staying stuck. And that is the cold, hard truth. Which may explain some of the resistance you are feeling as you outgrow people in your life. Turns out, a leopard does not change its spots. Because that is a leopard; we are people. Creations, made by a Creator, who are supposed to evolve and grow and outgrow and learn.

It is not that I had had a bad childhood. But when you grow up feeling not good enough for someone who contributed to your creation on earth, it manifests insecurities that breathe negative outcomes throughout your life until you become self-aware enough to do something about it.

Things that helped me:

1. **Every day, I wrote in *Start Today Journal* that "I speak with kindness and edification" until it was something I was confident I could say was truth.** When you start writing things down about yourself you wish were true, it holds you accountable to find ways to show up as that version of you. I don't always hit the mark and do it perfect with a pretty little bow on the end of each day. But I do make a conscious effort to speak in kindness and edification in every conversation I have. That doesn't mean that I forsake the boundaries I've established. It just means that I have to make it a priority before entering a conversation to meditate, pray, and practice what it is I want to say, to ensure that I am doing my best to be kind in my speech.

2. **Practice makes progression.** The more you practice speaking truth in kindness and with love, it becomes easier. The more you focus on how Jesus would respond, it paves the way for the Holy Spirit to work it out in you, and give you the words that you need. Jesus spoke boldly. He also spoke in love. He had no qualms with calling people out and questioning their faith and how they were behaving to make it a teachable moment. It was edifying. When He defended the whore in the town square to the Pharisees and said that "he who is without sin shall cast the first stone", He then turned to *her* and said, "now go and sin no more." He stuck up for her while also correcting her in love.[2] We don't have to get it right all the time; God knows we aren't perfect. It's the task of at least trying to be more like Christ that's the most important.

3. **This is still a work in progress.** Like I said before, I don't always hit the mark. Some days are fantastic, and I can lay my head on my pillow at night happy with how I handled every hard conversation or altercation. Other days, there is more grace and self-forgiveness than I'd care to admit, as well as some apologizing for when I've spoken out of my new character. It's the daily effort in being better that counts most when the day is done. If you can say at the end of each day that you showed up as your best self, put in the effort, and can be marked down as *present,* then you're headed in the right direction of progressing as a human.

CHAPTER 5

Deliverance

When I was in my early twenties, I met a guy. It was very much the school-girl crush kind of thing. He worked in the main office where I worked. I was constantly waiting for him to walk down the pathway or come out the door to the smoking area at break. It was the kind of crush that made me want to do whatever I could without making a fool out of myself to find out his name and try to catch a glimpse of him. After a few weeks of playing coy and doing what I could to look cute at work to catch his eye, he noticed me, and we started talking. Then, we started dating. Then, we got serious. My parents were not keen on him at all. He was not impressive by their standards, which should have spoken volumes to me, but being a naïve twenty-something, it did not matter to me. I was going to do what I was going to do. Mere months into our relationship, we were talking about moving in together. This went over exactly like I thought it would when we talked to my parents and got their feedback. It was a disaster. They were adamantly against it. So, I did what any brat would do who did not get what she wanted. I packed my stuff and left while my mom was at work, leaving her only a note. It broke her heart. It broke my dad's heart. It probably left my brother confused and hurt, too. It broke my heart. I didn't want to leave like I did, but I also knew that at the time, I wanted a place of my own with my new guy. I cried the whole car ride to our apartment. He shared the apartment with a roommate, for the record. We eventually got our own place. My parents came to visit and tried to be as kind and supportive as possible, given the circumstances. They always reassured me that I would have a place if things did not work out. And I knew they truly meant it.

Somehow, we naively went into this new venture of a shared apartment without really having a great financial plan. We borrowed money from his mom for the down payment that was required for the landlord, and I was on the lease as a qualified occupant, because my credit was too bad to have my name put on the contract. We were off to a great start. I really hope you caught the sarcasm there.

It started out not too bad, in all honesty. But I went from *not too bad* to bad. Then, bad got worse.

He was on prescription pain killers from a car accident that injured his back. He'd been on them for some time, and when you're on prescription opiates for an extended period of time, your body builds up a tolerance, making it so that you have to take more than what has been prescribed by your doctor to help the pain. And when you take more than what the prescription indicates, you run out of medication before it is allowed to be refilled per the insurance. This is because it was an opiate, which is a controlled substance. Meaning that the pharmacy has the right to refuse refilling it or they can bypass the insurance and let the patient pay out of pocket.

There are a lot of hoops to jump through. And it is for the patient's safety to refuse refilling it. It also means that the patient can take their prescription to another pharmacy. But that is simply not good enough, because those patients become addicted. I mean, it is a controlled substance for a reason. As the insurance would not cover the refill, and pharmacies were refusing to fill the prescription, he got tired of being in pain and in withdrawal. I do not exactly remember how he got the connection, but he found someone about a half hour away from where we lived who sold Oxycontin out of their house. How that happens is someone gets a large prescription each month from their doctor and turns around to sell them on the street. It quickly turned from getting Vicodin from his doctor to getting Oxycontin from a dealer. At some point, taking them by mouth with water was no longer doing the trick. That led to them being crushed and snorted up a rolled-up dollar bill.

Then, he offered it to me to "try". At first, I declined. I was taught about this in D.A.R.E. I knew better. I was raised better. But then, it was offered again. So, I tried it. "Just to see what it was like," I said.

Once led to twice. Twice led to a third. Then, l was hooked. Before we knew it, we were getting prescription pills for the both of us, and it was becoming expensive. We still had rent to pay and groceries to buy, not to mention gas and cigarettes. As it became more and more costly to keep up with our habit, we found out that heroin does the same thing as Oxycontin, and it costs a lot less. So, we found a heroin dealer who was a just a few miles further than our pill dealer. Then, things got worse. Much worse. It went from recreational usage to addiction in a matter of days for the both of us. Before we knew it, we were faced with being late on rent and borrowing more money from his mother to cover the cost of living. That led to him going to payday loan businesses weekly to get an advance on his paychecks to help fund our cost of living. Rent. Food. Smokes. Gas. Drugs. It was getting out of hand. So out of hand that we were getting payday loans to pay back payday loans, so we could have enough from our paychecks to live off of. All because of a drug addiction.

Not only was it taking control of our finances, it was taking control of our lives. Neither of us could go to work without using first. We also had to take some with us to help get us through the shift when it started to wear off. It was seeping into our judgement and behavior. Things that were out of character and that would cost me my job. I was stealing money just to support our habit and have money for dinner that week. Addiction is a bitch. It makes people do things they would not normally do to keep from getting sick and being able to function. It tears apart families and destroys lives. It claims not only their character but can also claim their lives.

Overdose after overdose, I found myself on the bathroom floor. Laying on the cold tile after having thrown up for the fifth time because I had snorted too much. I overdosed over 100 times. Every night, at least twice, for eight months. The last night that I overdosed, I recall looking in the mirror. My pupils were so dilated that I could not see the green in my eyes. I remember being so ashamed of what I had become. I remember the feeling of shock, horror, and embarrassment I felt I was bringing to the Mason name by the life I was living as a heroin addict. I also remember God Almighty reaching down to me while I was in the pit and pulling me out. I remember feeling such a freedom when I looked in the mirror and said, "No more."

With all the will, courage, and strength I could muster up, I walked back into our bedroom and laid down on the bed. I told him that I couldn't do it anymore. I had to stop using. He replied with, "Okay, but I have to for my back," or something like that. I honestly don't remember his exact response. I knew that if I was going to stand firm in my decision to stop using, I couldn't be around him when he was. After having that conversation with him, I moved to sleeping on the couch. I was in withdrawal and not feeling so hot, but I knew I was stronger, because the Lord was giving me the strength. Even though I was not using, it was still a struggle to keep up with the bills, and we were behind on some things.

It had gotten to such a financial struggle that I did not have the money to pay my car insurance, causing it to lapse. Since my place of employment was a five-minute drive—including stoplights—from our apartment, I drove uninsured for weeks, maybe even a few months.

Then, the night that God orchestrated to rescue me from the abyss came.

My boyfriend and I went to Wendy's to grab food. I drove, because it was not far, and his car was a mess on the inside. We sat in the drive-thru waiting for our food, and a police officer pulled up behind us. He ran my plates just for fun. At least I am guessing it was just for fun. We no sooner got our food than the red and blue lights started flashing in my rear view. As the "Oh crap" left my mouth, a prayer of gratitude went up to Heaven that we did not have any drugs on us.

My car was towed. My then-boyfriend walked back to get his car to pick me up. We both needed some time to process what was happening, and then, we went home. That night, we knew that things were going to change. We did not have the money to get my car out of repossession. We did not have money for court costs for me to go before a judge and testify as to why I was driving without insurance. A lot of things were piling up all at once.

I called my mother. I told her what had happened, and that I needed to come home. The next day, I packed some things and left while he was at work.

Weeks passed, and I showed up for court, got things ironed out with the law, and finished getting my things from the apartment. We tried to work things out. He could not stay clean, and I had a list of things nearly a mile long that he needed to change for us to be able to be together.

After an extremely hard but honest and necessary conversation, we broke up.

Like any other breakup, it was hard. Was I broken-hearted? Yep. But I was ready to move on from such a hard time in my life. I had given so much of myself to someone that not, only had I started to lose who I was, I was so far removed from the person I thought I was. I was ready to rediscover myself again. I was ready to figure out what I wanted since it was clear that I knew what I didn't want.

Months had gone by, and even after breaking up with my boyfriend, losing driving privileges, moving back in with my parents, and having to find a new job, I did not have a single relapse.

 But I did have a substitution.

I traded heroin for pot.

My withdrawals were horrible the first few weeks, and after I had moved back home, I did not know anyone who sold heroin. However, I did know a ton of people who would sell me some weed. Hindsight tells me that was a blessing in disguise. Who knows where I would be today if I had still been using?

I would not be writing this story, nearly twelve years from being *delivered* from a heroin addiction.

I say 'delivered' because Jesus saved me. Nearly twelve years without one relapse. I white-knuckled through my withdrawals. I stood my ground with my boyfriend, who had become my enabler. I got clean on my own with no one to help but the Savior, who had paid the ultimate price for me to be free.

Who the Son sets free, is free indeed.[1]

1. **I learned what I didn't want in a partner.** I had a decent idea as to what I didn't want in partner, based on what I had gone through, which paved the way for me to start learning what I *did* want. I still wasn't sure at the time how to find that person, but having a good idea of the things I wasn't willing to tolerate made for a good blueprint to start with.

2. **I started to integrate myself back into the church.** I started going back to church on a regular basis. Growing up in faith, I knew it was where I should be, needed to be, and where I would find my healing. I was still smoking pot, so I was very much serving two masters, but that is the thing about Jesus. He accepts and loves you as you are, and works in you, and your heart, to clean out the hurt, pain and suffering over time. He, too, was hurt, beaten and bruised.[3] He is the wounded Healer.

3. **I surrounded myself with people who were in church.** Proximity is power.[4] Scientific research proves that you are a combination of the five people you surround yourself with. I was spending equal time with people who worshipped Jesus and people who smoked weed. This made it easy for me to remain stuck in that situation of

serving myself while praising God. All the justifications and excuses of self-medicating for the sake of staying off hard-core heroin or "self-medication" throughout the years, were no match for the purpose my Lord had over my life. The more I surrounded myself with people who were in church, the easier it became for me to give up smoking weed when it was time to let it go. Over time, it, too, had become a form of addiction I had to overcome. I had to be willing to let go of the world, in order to make an impact on it for Christ's sake.

CHAPTER 6

Paper Hearts

His name was John*. To be honest, his name is not John. But I made a promise when I started writing this book that names would be changed or kept quiet to protect the innocent and the guilty, and I have every intention of keeping that promise. Even though we have not spoken in years, and he has no idea I am about to tell the world what happened, integrity is what you do when no one is watching. So, like a Reba McEntire song, his name is John.

He was the first man I dated as an adult that I could see myself marrying. All the other men I had dated were not the kind that I could see myself with in the future. I could not imagine my life without him. He lived in Michigan and had two kids of his own and was also in the middle of a divorce. He had been unfaithful, and his wife could not forgive him. Understandably so. They were in the middle of custody battles and court hearings when we met. To be honest, I do not remember exactly how we met. My initial guess is online dating.

I know what you are thinking. "Hannah, he's married, still. And living in another state. What are you thinking?"

I was not thinking. They say love is blind. It is not. Love is a choice. Lust makes you do dumb things. Lust controls your feelings and thought process, making it nearly impossible for you to think clearly. I was in actual love. I chose to be with someone who had cheated on his wife and was still married. I chose to be with someone, despite logic telling me otherwise. I remember talking on the phone for hours every day. Exchanging text messages all day. As time moved our relationship on, we made plans for the future. He drove down to Ohio every other weekend to see me. I fell hard and fast. We had even gotten to the place in our relationship where he wanted to put me on a shared cell phone plan with him, so we could FaceTime at night. He bought me a phone and had me added to his plan. I thought it was just another step in the right direction of our blooming relationship.

There were so many red flags I naïvely ignored, like how I thought I would be different than his wife, the woman to whom he was still legally married. He had been unfaithful to this wife—with a woman he had met on a church mission trip, no less! Or the time I went to visit him in Michigan, and he did not want to introduce me to his kids, despite having met my son. How, when I went to visit, he put me up in a hotel room, instead of allowing me to stay with him at his parent's house, like he got to when he came to visit me. Yes, he was living with his parents. To be honest, so was I at the time. So, Pam, quit judging. What seemed to justify things for me, at the time, was that he was in the church. He seemed desperate to be forgiven and wanted to right his wrongs. He seemed like he was trying to change and get on the right track. Another thing that should have been a red flag was how he would buy me lingerie for every landmark anniversary we hit, or for my birthday. Seeming like he was trying to change, and actually changing are two different things. Someone who is in the church will lead you closer to Jesus, not closer to sin.

So many red flags I did not pay any attention to, because I chose to ignore them. I remember my mom making a statement to me that made me start to question everything, "I hope you're not the rebound." I hoped so, too.

The one red flag that ended up being the one I could not ignore was the time I went to visit for a weekend, and he showed me his new office space. He had just started renting an office for his practice as a child counselor. As I observed his new space, one particular picture on his bulletin board caught my eye. It was a strip from a photo booth session he'd gone on with his wife and kids. The part that struck me was that it had his soon-to-be ex-wife in them. He tried to play it off, stating that it was the only pictures he had of his children. I do not know if he thought I was that stupid, or if he thought he was that good of a liar. I was not buying it. My immediate thought was, *you can't tell me your school-aged kids don't have school pictures taken.* I did not say it out loud. I did not want to make it any worse than what it was. He could clearly see that I was upset by it. We got into a huge argument on the way back to my hotel room —the biggest fight we had ever had. He admitted to grieving the loss of the family he once had. I understood that. I respected that. What I did not get was why he felt the need to lie about it until I called him out on it during our blow up. We tried to reconcile that night and save the trip. He took me home the next day. It was the most awkward and painful car ride of my life. I tried to process how I felt, what had happened, and where we were to go from there. Thinking it wasn't what it was, though it was exactly what it was. I was *the rebound.* I was no different than all the other women he cheated on his wife with. I was something to fill the time. Something to distract him. Whereas for me, he was the man I thought I would one day marry. I let him into my home, my family, my heart. I let him into my life, just to be the rebound. The placeholder. The same was never done in return for me. I wasn't let into his life like he was into mine.

Over the coming weeks, things were really starting to change between us. I began to lose trust in him, because he had lied about something that I would have been able to understand and empathize with. I started tracking him on the Find My iPhone app when he said he was at work late, claiming that as the excuse for why he hadn't called.   Things just didn't feel right.

I could see that he was not at his office. I could see that he was not being truthful. Every time I had asked, he had no problem either ignoring me or making up a story to delay having the hard conversation that he had found someone else.

When I found out he was cheating on me, I was broken-hearted. You would think that it was something I would have seen coming, considering how it was what he had already done to his wife. You would think I would not have been so surprised. I was, because I was not paying attention to all of the red alerts that were worthy of paying attention to.

I was willing to look past all the signs because I thought I had found "the one".

After we broke up, I went into a state of depression, one like I had not been in before. I was living in complete apathy. I cared about a total of two things: keeping my son alive and keeping my job. During the mourning phase of the aftermath of a gut-wrenching breakup, I felt the way most women feel after they've had their hearts ripped out of their chest, thrown on the concrete, and run over by a Mac truck – like I would never love again.

How could I? The love I had for him was all-consuming. It was lust plus love. The ultimate combination of all-consuming, without a doubt, life-changing love. And I was grossly aware of how I had never felt that way about someone before. All the past relationships I had been in could not compare to this one. The one where I felt like I had met the man I would wake up and fall asleep next to every day for the rest of my life. And he was gone, forever removed from my life, and there was nothing I could do to get him back. Not a thing.

It was over. As Dr. Meredith Grey would say, "So over."

It was a place I never thought I would be in again, considering that I thought I had met the man I was going to marry. What I ended up learning was priceless.

Do not introduce your kids to someone that you *think* you are going to marry. Wait until you *know*. Also, the red flags are there for a reason. Pay attention to them. Do not let yourself get so engulfed in the fiery flames of love that you become ignorant to the warning signs flashing in red. They are flashing at you for a reason. Do not ignore them.

Turns out, my son had gotten attached, too. So not only was I grieving, I also had to explain to my four-year old every time he asked about John that we were not friends anymore, and we would never see him again. Oh, what fun that was. He was sad. What made matters worse was that he had a Build-A-Bear that John had gotten him on an outing to the mall we made as "a family" one day. You know how when you make a bear, they give you a heart with a real heartbeat to put inside when you are about to get it stuffed? The heartbeat was John's, and my son had a great attachment to that bear. A tangible reminder every day that it did not work out like I hoped, prayed, and dreamed it would. The ultimate gut-punch. It broke my heart all over again every time I saw that bear.

The bear eventually "got lost". #SingleMomInitiative.

Months went by, and just when I thought I was finally starting to really move on from John and the pain from our gut-wrenching breakup, I saw his face on social media, with the woman I assume he cheated on me with- BECAUSE THEY WERE MARRIED. It was a joint account. Of course, it was, he was a cheater. How could she fully trust him?

But then again, maybe she could trust him, and that's why she married him. Who knows? I know she knew about me, because she told him to remove me from the shared phone plan shortly after we broke up.

It had been merely five to six months since he and I had broken up, and I was now seeing his face on Facebook with a new wife in their wedding attire.

I was the ultimate rebound for him. The one that held the space for him to find someone he could let into his life the way I wanted to be.

To be honest, it was bittersweet. I felt gutted and relieved at the same time. Like I had dodged a bullet, but had my heart trampled at the same time. I don't think Webster's has a word to fully articulate how I felt when I saw them together. He felt so close, but so far away.

I told my mom. I was brave on the outside. Behind closed doors, I cried.

I stalked their joint account enough to discover that they had gotten engaged a month after he and I split. One whole month. Engaged. I don't know if he was seeing us both at the exact same time the whole time and she was who he chose, or if it started after the debacle in his office that fateful weekend. I don't know if she was one of the women he cheated on his first wife with and then they got back together. I don't know, and I don't think I want to. Sometimes, you do not need all the answers to find the closure you need to move on. Sometimes, there is no closure. Sometimes, you just lick your wounds and keep moving. Sometimes, you just have to keep going and only look back long enough to catch a glimpse of the life you would not have wanted to live. Even though it is what you thought you wanted, God always has something better in mind. It is always better than what you have imagined for yourself.

Something tells me he has been unfaithful to her, too. Something tells me that he is just not the one-woman kind of man. I hope

I am wrong. I hope he has evolved and changed and grown as a man, father, and person. I hope he is faithful to her. Because regardless of whenever she came along, no one deserves that level of pain. I hope he is not like the leopard that does not change its spots. I hope he is like the human that grows and evolves into a better version for his wife and kids. I want that for him, and them.

Things that helped me:

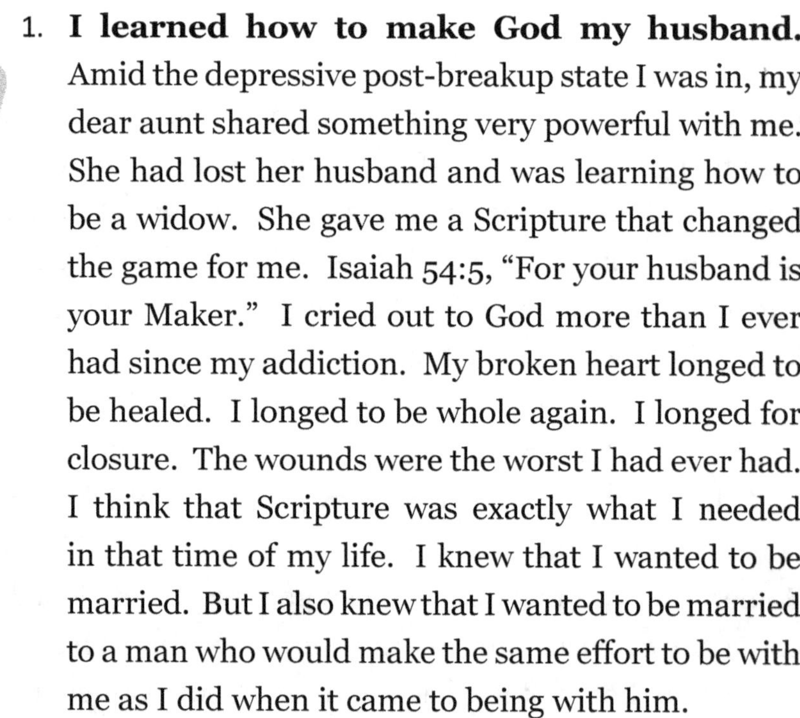

1. **I learned how to make God my husband.** Amid the depressive post-breakup state I was in, my dear aunt shared something very powerful with me. She had lost her husband and was learning how to be a widow. She gave me a Scripture that changed the game for me. Isaiah 54:5, "For your husband is your Maker." I cried out to God more than I ever had since my addiction. My broken heart longed to be healed. I longed to be whole again. I longed for closure. The wounds were the worst I had ever had. I think that Scripture was exactly what I needed in that time of my life. I knew that I wanted to be married. But I also knew that I wanted to be married to a man who would make the same effort to be with me as I did when it came to being with him.

2. **I realized there would never be closure.** Closure is something that is not always guaranteed. Sometimes, you do not get the answers to your *whys*

and *whens*. Sometimes, you do not get to speak your piece. Sometimes, you just have to lick your wounds and get back up. Sometimes, you just have to keep going and thank God for not answering your prayer in the way you wanted it answered. I used to not believe in unanswered prayers. I used to believe that God always answers prayers. I still believe that He does. But He does not answer them the way we want him to. Some of God's greatest gifts, are, in fact, unanswered prayers. If He had not ripped John away from me like He did, I wouldn't have the husband I have now. He is the true answer to my prayer.

3. **I learned how to let it go.** Sans closure, with a broken heart. It took time. A lot of time. A lot of tears. A lot of brave faces in public and on social media. I don't believe in "fake it 'til you make it". That is the most garbage advice in the Universe. FACE it until you make it. Keep showing up as who you wish you could be in that moment. Whether it is brave, healed, fantastic, or just okay, act the way you want to feel, until it is how you are. I do not mean bury your emotions, either. Feel those feelings. Allow yourself to process the hurt and seemingly irreparable pain. It is healthy and necessary. But when you are in public, around your kids, on social media, put on the armor of a well-dressed warrior. When you are alone or with your best pal is where you can be the most authentic form of you, in order to process in a healthy manner the way you are really feeling. Why? Because that is where it is safest. Because in the public platforms of the real world and on social media, there people who are looking to see how you are going to respond and act in specific situations. If you have kids, they

are watching you to see how you are doing and showing up in amid the suffering. Eventually, you will be okay. Eventually, you will be healed and whole and well. It will take time. Give yourself grace.

CHAPTER 7

Two Halves do not Make a Whole

There were a few fellas I casually dated or entered relationships with after John. None of them were what I wanted in a partner long term, until I met my now-husband. But this chapter is not about him.

Every guy that I entangled myself with one way or another after John and before Lenin, was, ultimately, a version of a rebound. Mostly, it was to occupy my time or distract me from the pain I was trying to heal. If you have ever watched *Sex and the City* for any length of time, you have heard this bit before, as stated by the notorious Samantha Jones, "the best way to get over someone is to get under someone else."

Not the worst piece of advice, but certainly not one I would give to my friend. No offense, Samantha—I just see myself as more of a Charlotte.

It is not the worst advice ever, because it helped me in a time of my life when I needed to know I was not numb. I needed to know that I could feel. That my heart still worked. That I was not someone who had lost all sense of feeling, purpose, and capacity to love.

The guy that I dated shortly before I met my husband proved to me that I could love again. I learned that my heart could beat for someone again. That I still had the desire to be a wife. He also taught me the most valuable lesson of all, two halves do not make a whole. Jerry Maguire messed all of us up. You do not complete anyone, and no one can complete you. You must be whole before you can be with someone you can spend the rest of your life with. You cannot enter a relationship or partnership not fully whole and healed and well and expect someone else to be the piece that makes you well. It will not work out. I know this because I used to think the same.

Every relationship in or casual dating partner I was with before I met my husband was proof of such theory.

When they say, "you cannot love someone until you learn to love yourself", find me, so I can slap them. That is garbage. My mom loved me when I did not love myself. Jesus loved me when I did not love myself. The actual thing you need to hear is this: you cannot be with someone until you can be with yourself. If you make a list of all the things you want in a life partner, make sure you have those qualities. I do not know what your list looks like. Mine was: self-sufficient, honest, godly, and a good listener, amongst other qualities. Those are things I was looking for, and I was not going to find them in someone if I did not have those on my own personal résumé. If you are looking for someone that is going to "fix" you, look in the mirror. If you are looking for someone to make you whole, look in the mirror. You are the one who needs to be able to be with you.

"How you feel about yourself when you are by yourself is the gap you need to close" was something Dave Hollis , author of *Get Out of Your Own Way* said in a book club meeting once, and it rings true here.

Have you ever heard the age-old saying, "You can't be with someone until you can be by yourself."?

That is capital 'G' Gospel truth.

I tried so hard, for so long to be with someone in order to fill my time or distract myself from the feeling of empty loneliness. The truth is, solitude is the best way for you to discover what you need to work on within yourself, before you can go and try to offer up anything you can give to someone else. You cannot be anything for someone else unless you can be that for yourself.

Stop trying to fill the void with things and people that are not going to help you transform into the person that you want and need to be. Stop sitting at the table when respect is no longer being served. Stop eating lunch with people who make you the topic of conversation when you get up to use the restroom. Stop shrinking yourself to fit into a mold that you have outgrown. Stop making people a priority when they only have you as an option. And most importantly, start making yourself a priority.

Eleanor Roosevelt is noted for saying that you cannot pour from an empty cup. You cannot walk through life expecting to be something for other people and expecting others to be what you need, when you are broken and hurting.

Relationships, romantic or otherwise, are not 50-50. Where that gets twisted is when people do not stop to realize that it is two people bringing to the relationship all of their effort, and in wholeness. You are not half of a whole. You are a whole, meeting someone halfway and putting in one hundred percent of your effort. It is compromise — give and take— on both sides, with mutual understanding of what the expectations are in that relationship.

Don't get it twisted. Friends with benefits is not a relationship, and very seldom will it turn into one that has more to offer than sexual gratification. When you start a relationship on the precedent of sex, do not expect anything more when it comes to feelings and commitment. Chances are, you are their rebound while they are on the mend.

Chances are you have read the book—or have seen the movie—*He's Just Not That into You* in the early 2000s. If he is not willing to fully commit, he is just not that into you, and you need to move on. Darling (in my Moira Rose voice), learn from my mistakes. Do not make someone a priority who is making you an option. You deserve more than to be a letter on a multiple-choice pop quiz.

I am not pretending to be a relationship expert or know the ins-and-outs of how to be a phenomenal wife. But I have learned a thing or two, because I have been through it. Whatever season you find yourself in when it comes to dating and relationships, I have been there.

I have been the other woman. I have been the friend with benefits who got too attached and ended up hurt. I have been the girl who thought she found the guy she was going to marry. I have been single, lonely, and hurt. I have done the dumping and been the one that is been dumped. I have cheated, been cheated on, and helped them cheat.

Side note: there is never justification or reasoning for cheating on any level. It is distasteful from every angle and not something of which I am proud. But I am grateful that it was a lesson that helped me learn who I did not want to be, and taught me the type of person I did not want to be with, based on how crappy it made me feel. The age-old phrase "once a cheater, always a cheater" is false. A tiger may not change its stripes, but a person can change who they are and learn from their mistakes.

Evolution may be a theory when it comes to animals, but it is proven that humans can grow, change, and evolve. I am proof of such evolution. God has done exemplary work in me over the years. But I have also done the assigned soul-work and learned the required self-awareness in those lessons. God can do anything, but He only goes so far if you are not willing to put in effort. He is a gentleman, never forcing Himself or His agenda on anyone who is not willing to receive it. There is a passage of Scripture that talks about weak flesh, but a willing spirit.[1] You have to be willing in your heart to do the work to make change for God to work in and through you.

1. **I realized that no one could be for me what I could not be for myself.** No one can complete you. You were given everything you needed when you were born. You are fearfully and wonderfully made.[2] "You were given worth at your birth, and no one can take that away from you." When Trent Shelton said that at a personal development conference I attended, I was floored. *Pedal to the metal* floored. It rang true for the insecurities I was feeling then, and it rings true here. You do not need anyone to bring you to completion. Jesus does that.[3] You do not need anyone to be your better half. You must be your better whole. Better half is a myth. That implies that people need someone to bring out the best in them and be the better part of their relationship. If you cannot be the best for yourself or be the best you for you to live the life you are made to live, you are not going to find it in someone else. Two halves do not make a whole when it comes to relationships. It is two whole people, coming together to live in wholeness with each other. I know at times you feel as though you are not enough. It is a lie; you were given worth at your birth. God didn't give Eve to Adam because he needed someone to make him whole. He gave him Eve as a companion to share life.

2. **No one could complete me, except Jesus.** Everyone knows that infamous line in *Jerry Maguire* when Tom Cruise tells Renée Zellweger "you complete me". "Gag me with a spoon", as they used to say in *Valley Girls*. Anyone familiar with Moon Zappa will get this reference. No one could complete me and make me whole and healthy enough to be in a healthy and functioning relationship. The idea of being completed by someone begs for the thought that we are not whole to begin with. If we aren't whole, we are broken. Go get fixed before entering a relationship that will not require some form of co-dependency. No wonder all my relationships failed up until I met my husband. I was dependent on other men to be what I needed when, in fact, God was all I needed. I did not come to this realization until I learned to fully depend on Him to be all that I needed. Then, I went from brokenness to wholeness. I went from being someone who would be dependent on another human for my happiness, to being someone that only needed Jesus to fulfill me. If you feel that you need someone to make you whole, consider how you may be broken and get to working on yourself, FOR YOURSELF.

3. **My "baggage" would always be there.** I will always have battle scars. As will you. We have wounds from the wars we have fought in life. That is the price of admission for living a life of curiosity and perseverance. I will always be someone who was raped. I will always be someone who had feelings of being abandoned by my biological father. I will always be someone who used to be a heroin addict. I will always be a mother to a child whose father was not the role model I'd like for him to have been. Baggage comes with life. It does not

mean you are less worthy of having happiness and hope. Or a future so bright you need sunglasses to envision it. What it does mean is that your wounds will heal, and they will become your battle scars. They become your lessons on how to live life. Tony Bennett said in a documentary once that life teaches how to live it if you live it long enough. That is so true, sweet reader. Your wounds will heal, if you give them the time they need to be raw and be kind enough to yourself for them to close. Battle scars never stopped being sexy.

CHAPTER 8

40z. to Freedom

I had a casual relationship with alcohol. I would go out with friends in my early twenties, like all young folks do, and hit up the local B-Dubs or hit the house party, then crash on someone's couch. During the week, I went to work, got on my hustle and grind, and when Friday came, I was on the road to my best friend's house to hit up the night life. It was glorious. At the time. Some of the best times I ever had were when she and I were together. We were connected at the hip—two peas in a pod. She is probably the only person, besides my husband, whose name I could keep in this book without editing, because she is that incredible and special to me. Time has since moved us on, and in different directions, and though we keep in touch, we do not have the same closeness. And that is okay. She is a lifelong friend, and I am grateful for the memories we share. We can meet for lunch or chat on the phone and still pick up right where we left off. Even if some of them are blurry and are going to be called into question when I am at the Judgement Throne of Christ. Pray for me.

I would often go to local bars or house parties hosted by people in my town. I would sneak alcohol into my house when I still lived with my parents because it was "their house, their rules", and alcohol caused gasps, head shakes, and lectures I did not want to hear. I remember one night in particular, New Year's Eve 2015. I had a bottle of champagne in my bedroom where my child was sleeping, and I was up late waiting for Dick Clark to drop the ball. I popped the champagne bottle, and the loud unleashing of the cork did not cause my parents to come upstairs, although I am sure they heard it. It did wake my child from his slumber long enough for him to ask what the noise was, and I pulled some lie out of thin air that was sufficient enough to get him to lay back down. "Mommy just opened something, and it fell, sweetheart." Not exactly the truth, but enough omission of details for it to constitute as lying by omission.

Side bar: I am the "frank parent". I told my child at a young age that there was no Easter Bunny, no Santa, and no Tooth Fairy. Some mom, by the name of Karen with a bad haircut, just had a heart attack. I never once believed it robbed him of his childhood or stole his innocence. He still gets presents on Christmas and an Easter basket on Easter morning. He still has fun trying to guess what is in the nicely wrapped packages under the tree and decorating cookies. He knows the truth of why we observe and celebrate the holidays we do in our faith.

Back to the drinking.

At the time, I did not consider the sneaking of alcohol to be a problem, other than it violated the rules of the house I was living in. Looking back, literally as I write these words, I am now seeing that even though it may not have seemed like an issue to raise concern then, it only contributed to me knowing how to sneak alcohol into my day without getting caught. Cork popping or not. As time moved on, I remained in a casual relationship with alcohol. It was not something I needed to be able to function and get through the day, and I recovered from hangovers like a champ. By that I mean, I rarely had them. Like, ever. I could take it or leave it when it came to drinking. There was a time when I did not drink at all or would casually have one drink at a luncheon or dinner setting. It was not until after I got married that my drinking escalated to being problematic. It had been about two-and-a-half years into our marriage that the drinking escalated. I was able to casually have a glass of wine with neighbors and at brunch on the deck and be fine. It was when that casual glass turned into a habitual glass— that habitual drink in the afternoon or the evening, lead to polishing off a whole bottle by myself. Or downing a six pack of beer without saving any for my husband, leaving it up to him to go get more from the store if he wanted any, because (1) I had drunk it all, and (2) I was too drunk to drive by 5:00 p.m. The normalization of day drinking only fueled the fire. When I saw memes and hashtags about how mommy needs wine, I felt justified in drinking to the excess that I was. It was not only justifying my drunkenness; it was also giving me permission to drink too much. Just before we moved from Columbus, Ohio to Pennsylvania is when the drinking really got out of hand. I remember pouring a glass of Winking Owl cabernet into a coffee mug at 11:00 a.m. and taking it out back to have with a cigarette. The cigarette served two purposes. The first was how much people who drink and smoke enjoy a cigarette with their drink.

The second was to help cover up my breath from smelling like dry red wine before noon. The coffee mug served two purposes, as well. The first was to hide from my husband that I was drinking at 11:00 a.m. The second was to hide from the neighbors that I was drinking anything other than coffee to go with my brunch-time smoke. The mugs you see online that say, "may be drinking wine", are 100 percent truth. She *may be* drinking wine at 10:00 a.m., and the only ones who know are her and God Almighty— and maybe her children who can smell it on her breath. I know these things because I was that mom. The mom who felt the need to drink to help myself parent. The mom who drank to help the day seem smoother and more fun. The mom who drank to help escape the non-stop demands of all the things that come from not only being a mom, but a woman who has a family and a house to keep clean. Drinking was my way of escape and celebration, my anesthetic when I needed to numb the pain, or guzzle down some courage to approach a hard conversation with my husband.

Do not get this twisted— my husband is phenomenal. Our marriage is even more phenomenal. The mile marker in our early marriage where I was playing the role of the drunk college chick and the housewife is not because I was in a bad marriage. It because I was in a marriage and did not know how to be in a marriage. It was because I was broken in some parts of my own life, aside from him. It was from— get this— thinking I would feel more whole and complete. I was unhappy in life, not in my marriage. Although at times it was hard to tell the difference, hindsight tells me I was just unhappy in life. I was unhappy with who I was because I was unhappy with the life I was choosing to live. I knew there was more for me. I knew I was made for more than the life I was living. I knew there was more to my life than doing laundry and cleaning house and watching true crime shows. Although I still do all those things now, it does not feel like the chore it used to feel like. The kind that I needed to get drunk before sorting the darks from the whites and the delicates in separate baskets. They now feel like things to simply be checked off the to-do list while I also write this book, or hang out with my kid, or binge watch a series on Netflix with my husband while the dog takes up too much space on the sofa. I now live a life that I do not feel like I must escape in order to get through the day. Sure, things get tough. I do not want you to think that just because I live a life that is free from needing to self-medicate myself that hard times pass over me like the Jews in Exodus. Although I am covered in the Blood of the Sacrificial Lamb, I still go through hardships and trials. Do not get this twisted, sis. The thing is, now I have other tools in my belt to help me when the going gets tough. My neighbors may be able to attest to seeing me jump and dance around in my office to Pink or to "Mr. Brightside", by the Killers. My husband can tell you I have escaped to the garage and cried it out for a few minutes before getting back up and fighting for joy. My son can tell you that I dance and skip around the house to Mercy Me with hands raised to the Heavens in praise while tears stream down my face. Tears of pain and tears of joy. My husband can tell you that the times I have wanted to have a drink or smoke a cigarette or pack a bong, I lace up my Nike's and go on a run and rap along to Cardi B and get my honky-tonk on to Shania Twain. Sometimes, life is tough, but so am I. I serve a God who is bigger than my problems and more steadfast in the storm than an umbrella in a margarita. Plus, I don't wake up the next day with a headache and upset stomach. Once you reach a certain age, recovery from drinking the day or night before is much slower and a much more hard-knock life. Cue the cast from *Annie* in a Jay-Z video. If you got that reference, you are my people, and I am grateful you are in this space.

When we were getting settled into our new home in Pennsylvania, the drinking slowed down. I was getting excited that the hopes of a new life wouldn't make me feel like I needed to escape. Then, the drinking picked back up out of celebration, and also out of anxiety for the new life I was about to start living. Little did I know that alcohol is a depressant, and it also stifles your growth. It stifles growth because it keeps you numb. It keeps you in a daze and unable to obtain the benefits of facing hard things without the effect of toxins and mind-altering substances. I also was vaping THC. It is legal here. But that does not make it any less harmful to the body, the brain, or your personal growth. The liquid turned to the plant when the liquid was getting hard to obtain. That is still illegal where I live.

The combination of escalated drinking, pot consuming, and cigarette smoking was quickly looking like an old life that I used to live before I was married. Before I fully surrendered my life to Christ. Before I was the mother of a son who needed someone with more mental faculties than a stoned college chick who partied on the weekends to raise him up to be a decent human. It was stifling my growth, and I was not aware of the sabotage I was doing to myself. I could not grow into the person I was placed on this earth to be, because I was still behaving like I was on a clean version of *Girls Gone Wild*.

I should add that we moved to Pennsylvania because the Lord had laid on my heart and confirmed through prayer that this is where He wanted us to be, so we could spread the ministry of the Gospel and serve His Kingdom and His beloved people. This was off the cusp of me being catapulted into the personal development space by a cute blonde with hair extensions who had taken my world by storm. *Girl, Wash Your Face* was the single most influential piece of literature I had ever read and was the catalyst for change I was looking for in a life where I felt like I was losing myself in the piles of laundry and bottles of house cleaner, with a side car of cheap wine from Aldi. I gobbled up that book within a matter of two days and was ready to take control of the things in my life that I could control, even though I had no idea how. Thankfully, *Girl, Stop Apologizing* was released not long after Rachel Hollis worked her magic and had me ready to take charge and live the life I knew I was supposed to be living. Our decision to move to Pennsylvania came when I decided to wake up from the nightmare I was living called *my life.*

The time came for me to stop drinking when I started having those conflicting internal conversations with myself about how much I was drinking. If you are a drinker— or ever were a drinker— you know what I am talking about here.

Those internal dialogues are often a tug-of-war with how much you are drinking and comparing it to others, justifying it with celebrations and vacations, or giving yourself permission to enjoy one after a long day of whatever took up space on your calendar. The internal conversations where you promise yourself you will only have just a few and that you won't have a drink tomorrow.

Those conversations. Mine came in the form of justifying the need to have a drink as a way of coping or escaping, to numb or to celebrate— and I was celebrating too hard— or self-medicating to the point where it was too hard to handle. I had to have a hard talk with myself about how much I was drinking. It came in the form of, "if you don't get a handle on this, you will become an alcoholic." It also came in the form of realizing that my life could be what it is supposed to be if I were to cut alcohol out. That is a hard realization and a hard pill to swallow when you are self-medicating and numbing with a depressant that is also an addictive substance.

I did not know what a life without alcohol would be like, but I knew it was something I wanted to check out before my drinking got so much out of hand that I had to go to treatment or AA meetings. I had no idea what to do. I did not know how to even try to get a handle on my drinking problem when it was not at rock-bottom yet. I had hit rock-bottom in other areas of my life before. It is not hard to figure out how to come back from rock-bottom, because it is a requirement, unless you want to die. Drinking had not reached a point of no return, yet. Navigating that was going to be hard.

Then God.

God showed me how, in the way He always does. This time, He did it through the Hollis'. Dave and Rachel Hollis are gurus in the personal development space. They have products, podcasts and a huge fan base. They also used to have a morning show that streamed live on social media.

Anyway. One morning on the show, Dave mentioned something he had been writing down as a dream to make come true: that he can say that he hasn't had a drink in a year. *Holy guacamole.* A whole year without a sip of alcohol. There was no way that just the day before I was asking myself how I was going to get a handle on my drinking before it went too far. Of course. Write it down, as if it were true.

It is a goal-setting practice preceded by gratitude that I had been doing for some time, and will go into much more detail later, that has been 'all-caps' LIFE-CHANGING for me.

On August 2, 2019, I started writing down in my *Start Today* journal that I haven't had a drink in a year. By the time this book hits shelves, I will have surpassed that one-year mark, and I plan on celebrating with non-alcoholic champagne. That is a party I am excited to attend.

When people say that you are one choice away from living a different life, they are 100 percent accurate. It is a choice that is yours to make as to whether you stay in the stuck you cannot get out of, or you do something about it and make a change. Either way, you are making a choice. Be sure you choose wisely.

Ah, the beauty of free will. We are here for a purpose. It is whether we choose to do something with that purpose or stay in a place of living hell that is up to us.

Do not get this twisted. God is sovereign. He has a plan and a purpose for each of us. It is up to us to decide if we want to be who He calls for us to be, or if we want to stay in a place of complacency and doing what we want. I can assure you as a person who has had things my way and lived life as I wanted to, living it as He wants me to is exponentially better. I feel like I have a place and a purpose on this earth. I no longer feel like I am constantly searching for my "why", nor trying to fit in. I was never born to fit in. I was called to stand out. I was set apart[1] with a purpose and a mission over my life. I cannot even sit here and say that I only wish I had found it sooner. I was not supposed to find it sooner. I was supposed to find it exactly when I did, because if I had found it sooner, my testimony would not be as powerful as it is. I would not be able to grow as much as I have in the last year, or even the last six months if I had found my purpose sooner. There is no way that my Thursday night women's group meetings would be as powerful as they are if I had found things sooner.

A friend pointed something out to me today. She said that she thinks the biggest catalyst for change in my life was when I stopped drinking. She had learned from a mentor that in order to be someone who utilizes all your emotional and physical capacities, you cannot put any toxins into your body. Gospel truth, ladies and germs. Gospel.

I would never, *never* be able to do the things I do now if I had continued down the path I was headed. Aside from leading a women's group through my church or aspiring to one day preach a sermon from a pulpit, I could not be who I am today. I could not be in training for a marathon. I could not have the lung capacity and function if I had kept smoking like a freight train. I could not keep up with my son, the house, and a naturally energetic husband if I kept poisoning my body with toxins that are scientifically proven to destroy you.

Giving up drinking was one of the biggest catalysts for change I had experienced, after I had entered the personal growth space. All the gratitude, goal-setting, journaling, and book work I had been doing was leading me up to this point in my life where I could finally get out of my own way and take the final step into living out the purpose of my creation.

A sober minded, purpose-driven, overcoming badass who has an intrinsic desire to make an impact on women and help them reach for more in their own lives, regardless of the obstacles.

More than likely, I had climbed a similar mountain and slayed the same dragons. I wanted them to know that they could do it, too. I wanted to be the light at the end of their dark tunnel that resembled hope and a future that was only possible by God, Himself. I also wanted to encourage them to choose to use their free will to make more out of their own lives.

Things that helped me:

1. **I had to ask myself if my life would be better without alcohol.** The question had been proposed to me via social media. God works in mysterious ways and can use anyone or anything to get His message across. I was scrolling through Instagram, my true drug of choice, and a post had caught my eye. It proposed a hard reality I needed to ask myself: "It's not always about asking yourself if you're an alcoholic. Sometimes it's about asking yourself if your life would be better without alcohol." Pow, right in the kisser. (That's a Peter Griffin line, by the way.) I wish with all the wishes on a red-seeded dandelion that I could remember the account that posted it. To be honest, I was probably drunk when I read it, but none the less, it hit me like a ton of bricks and was the buzz kill I needed. I knew that if I did not get a handle on my drinking that I would become an alcoholic. I knew that it was not good for my mental and physical health. I knew that I was using it as a coping mechanism, and it was only going to get worse if I did not come to terms with how much I was leaning on it to help me get through the day. I meditated on that statement for less than five minutes, and I knew that the answer was "Yes". Yes, my life would be better without alcohol. Yes, it was a step I knew I needed to take. No, it was not something that I was ready to let go of, but knew that I would never be ready if I kept holding on. You

know the age-old quote that says it hurts more to hold on than it does to let go, that is where I was with drinking. It was going to hurt me more to keep drinking than it was to let go before I hit rock-bottom.

2. **I set a personal goal to go one year without a drink.** Not even a sip. Something that I do every single day, and mentioned earlier, is list goals that I have and things I am grateful for, in my journal. This practice has changed my life, and by the time this book hits shelves, I will be over 700 days in doing this life-changing work. I started to write that I have not had a drink in a year.   On August 2, 2020, I will be one year without a sip of alcohol. The mere thought makes me want to prematurely pop the non-alcoholic champagne bottle I have tucked in my refrigerator for this momentous occasion. What a milestone. Doing this simple act of writing it down every morning that I haven't had a drink in a year does two things: First, it holds me accountable for another day to not drink. Secondly, it rewires my brain, because I am feeding it goodness by positive words, as opposed to hoping that I can make it another day without feeling like I need a drink.

3. **I gathered tools to add in my toolbox to help when it became difficult to not have a drink.** Besides mentally holding myself accountable, I knew I would need true accountability. There are hundreds— if not thousands and millions— of sober accounts on social media to provide communities to those who are sober and looking to stay sober. Put yourself in community with people who are also sober to not only provide you with accountability, but also for

encouragement when times get tough. Find a substitute. You are going to want to drink shortly after you give it up. You are going to have to learn how to fight those urges, and one of the best ways is to find a substitute. It can be anything that is healthy. Prayer. Meditation. Dance parties. Exercise. Journaling. Pinterest rabbit holes. Ginger ale or tea. All of these are things I used when I needed a drink. Especially exercise. Running became my exchange token for drinking and smoking. I traded everything unhealthy for running. It was something I always wanted to be able to do and an identity I wanted to resonate with: a runner. It's so much more badass to say "I am a runner," instead of "I am an alcoholic."

4. **I had to rewire how I thought about drinking.** Instead of thinking that I *couldn't drink,* I had to start thinking that I *don't need to drink.* I don't need to reach for a drink to numb or escape or celebrate or cope or bring up the courage. I had to rewire how I talked to myself about coping with hard things, so I started writing, "I am dependent on Christ, alone." Meaning that my only sources of courage, strength, and celebration were prayer, praise, and worship. Do not get this twisted, I love to pray, praise, and worship. But that is not always the route I wanted to take those first few weeks. Telling myself that I was only dependent on Jesus held me accountable and rewired my thoughts when things got hard. The mind is incredible. To be honest with you, prayer was not always my go-to choice those first few weeks. It was much easier to smoke some weed (more on that later) or dance it out to Britney Spears. As the Pinterest worthy quote says, put your hair in a ponytail, get some Starbucks, put on some

Britney, and handle it. That was, and still is, my motto. Only now, there is prayer in between the ponytail and coffee.

Freedom

Shortly after I got married, I started to lose myself. I started to feel like my identity was being rooted in a laundry troll who cleaned the house, scrubbed toilets, and packed lunches. I had always been the girl who dreamed of the wonderful husband, with the house and kids, and the lifestyle of being a homemaker and a stay-at-home mom. It was modeled for me by my own mother, who was there when we got home from school and made dinner every night. She is the best, and as a child, I wanted to be just like her. She made everything look so easy, and I knew at a young age that I wanted to have that on my résumé as an adult.

Not a single soul knows the work involved with being a housewife and a stay-at-home mom except those who do it. It can be daunting to keep up with the laundry, constantly wiping and swiping counter tops, and sweeping floors that were just mopped the day before— or even the hour before. I see the memes on Facebook about why even bother cleaning when people still live there, and I laugh because I get the sentiment. Then, the clean freak, who was raised in a home that was *always* clean, comes out and immediately refutes such arguments in my head. I like a clean house, always have, and I always will. My mother will read this and recall the child who shoved things under her bed, and crammed clothes into the dresser drawers, to make her bedroom appear as clean as the rest of the house. I imagine she may chuckle at the previous statement. Allow me to rephrase, she had standards; I was lazy. Nonetheless, I still enjoyed and appreciated a clean home with fresh linens on the bed, and dusted shelves. Even when I was older, and my son and I lived with my parents, I tried to keep things tidy. They were not tidy to her standards, but we had a lot of stuff and not so much space.

When I had the divine opportunity to be home when my child returned from school, and cook dinner every night for my family, I jumped at the chance. I took the opportunity and relished in being able to keep up with the housekeeping and folding laundry while watching whatever my heart desired on the television. When I was growing up, I remember watching my mom fold towels and snap green beans to *The Young and the Restless*. For me, it was *Grey's Anatomy* or anything in the true crime genre. It was lovely. For a while. Then, my depression sank in, and it started to become hard to even change out of my pajamas to walk my son down to the bus stop. Or even put on real shoes to go outside. I always chose the knock off Uggs or flip-flops, because at times, the thought of lacing up sneakers was too much. Some days, it was hard to get out of bed or make myself take a much-needed shower. Those who live with debilitating depression know what I am talking about. Laundry would pile up, and I would cry at the thought of having to separate it into designated piles and haul it to the washer. I would become overwhelmed by the to-do lists and grocery shopping that waited for me that day. It was becoming more and more of something I begrudgingly did, instead of something I felt blessed to be able to do. I cannot imagine having a full-time job and having to scrub the toilets and cook dinner. Depression was something I struggled with as a young adult and would have to take medication to maintain. Albeit, I did not always take my medicine and do what I was supposed to do to take my mental health seriously, but I did become a master at wearing a mask and pretending to be okay when I was anything but.

When I met my now-husband in 2017, I was about a year without being medicated by prescription drugs and had stopped self-medicating with marijuana the previous year. I was active in my church and became an expert at living a life of faking it until I made it when it came to being happy. I wore a mask at work, home, and church and had gotten to a place in my life where I was even lying to myself about how I was feeling, in order to avoid having to go back on medication and seeing a therapist. There was still such a stigma around mental health that I did not want to identify with it, so I pretended it did not exist. I became the expert at smiling when I wanted to cry and holding back tears until I got to the bathroom or behind closed doors. That is no life to live. Fake it until you make it is garbage advice, because it gives the person permission to ignore what is really going on. The more you do it on a regular basis, the easier it is to dismiss that there is a real issue that needs to be dealt with.

When I met the man I knew I would marry, it was sublime being around him and talking to him. I had myself convinced that I was healed and cured by the power of love and that Jesus had healed my depression. Finally. Oh, how I was wrong. I had become so good at ignoring the issue and pretending to be okay that I had fooled myself in the worst way. Then, when life became more and more overwhelming, the true nature of my condition reared its ugly head. It wasn't that we had a bad marriage, please do not misconstrue that. It was that I HAD NEVER BEEN MARRIED BEFORE, let alone been in a relationship that was everything I had ever wanted when it came to being Godly and edifying to my walk with the Lord. Every past relationship was an example of two things, (1) what I did not want and (2) what God did not want, as described in His Word. I had truly *never* done this before. I had never been a wife before, let alone to a Godly man, living a fully surrendered life to the Lord. I had never not had to work outside of the house. I had never been loved by a man who loved Jesus first and was patient beyond all comparison. I had never been with someone who loved my child like his own. Ladies, especially single moms, hear me: THIS IS THE KIND OF MAN YOU ARE LOOKING FOR. It took me thirty-three years to find him; do not let go of hope.

All these unknowns paved the way for me to revert to old ways of coping, which happened to include marijuana and alcohol. My husband would enjoy a social drink or a glass of wine with me on occasion. He was never the kind to be abusive when it came to drinking. He never judged and always understood. When I knew I needed something for my depression and anxiety, I knew that I did not want to go to a doctor and be put on medication, because I had already gone that route and did not like how the medication made me feel like a zombie or a freakshow. Furthermore, it was expensive and not something we could afford without me having to go back to work. The only thing that I felt helped with my symptoms, and did not have adverse side effects, was marijuana. I knew I would have to somehow convince my God-fearing, Jesus-loving, Bible-preaching, law-abiding husband that this was the right choice. I presented my facts, medical history, and past experience, and he agreed that since it was for medicinal purposes, it was a sound choice to make. I can be very persuasive when I need to be. Not saying I could sell candy to a diabetic, but I could get them to sample it. A neighbor of ours smoked weed, so I knew I could get a connection from him. And I did. I also tapped into some connections in my hometown and had a few backup contacts. Any person who smokes pot, either medicinally or recreationally, has more than one connection. It is just smart smoking.

At any rate, *medicinally* eventually turned into addiction. I do not care who tells you that you cannot get addicted to pot. Hear it from the source: YOU CAN. You can even ask Google.

When I did not have it, I got irritable and had trouble sleeping. I had headaches and was the worst kind of company to be around. Even my appetite would cease to exist. Essentially, I was going through withdrawals. It would get to the point where I would scrape the resin out of my pipe just to have something to smoke when I had to wait for either payday or my connections. It is an addictive substance. And I became addicted. I was a pothead in every sense of the word.

It helped my mood and gave me the motivation to clean the house and sort laundry. It helped me find the determination to get up in the morning and take on the day. It helped me, but it did not help the unknowns of marriage. It caused fights and tension. It also caused me to feel insecure when talking to my husband about things going on in the house or internally. It helped, but it also hindered. It caused me to be apathetic toward how he felt about it over time, because my feeling better was the ultimate goal most days.

I fight tears as I realize this in hindsight.

How dare I do that to the man who has done nothing but care for me and try to understand. How dare I put him and our marriage in a place of tension and hurt. What kind of wife does that? What kind of mom does that? An addicted one.

Addiction knows no gender, race, tax bracket, or religious affiliation. It knows no boundaries, reason, or morals. Addiction is a synonym for apathy. It does not care.

It does not care about who it hurts, the relationships it destroys, or the person it takes over. Lines become blurred, and judgement gets called into question in its presence. It is a monster, a dragon, a demon. It is all-consuming and unforgiving.

I am, by no means, excusing my actions. I am, however, making it clear that my actions were done because I had an addiction to an addictive substance. I know in my heart there is no shame in that. But knowing such and taking the step to forgive myself are two different things. I am still working on the latter.

I was not proud of my identity. Although I was married to the man that was an answer to my prayers, and lived in a beautiful home, I was not living a life that I was happy about. The life I was living was not the one I had envisioned as a child. On the outside, it was grand. On the inside, it was anything but. I praise the good Lord that my child never saw the pain I was in or the hurt that was in our marriage because of my addiction. It was seemingly normal to my husband, and I justified my abuse of marijuana by saying that it was my medication for my mental illness.

Mental illness and mental health are two sides of the same coin. The wordage is in the eye of the beholder. Mental illness is just that: mentally ill. Mental health is just that: a healthy mind, despite having an invisible disease.

I was living such an unhappy life, that I had to get high or drink, sometimes both, to feel like I was happy in it. That is no life to live.

I did not become aware of my ability to do something about it until I read *Girl, Wash Your Face,* the catalyst for change that I needed to find it within myself to make change. The entire book was relatable in a way I had never experienced in literature before. If you have never read the book, , please do. Each chapter refers to a lie that women believe about themselves at some point in their life, and how to overcome that lie. It still is my favorite book of all time. Do not get this twisted: the Bible is every Christian's favorite book. But not everyone that reads the Bible become changed by the words so much that it becomes a compass for them to navigate life in each day. Scripture is riddled with encouraging words in adversity and how to live each day as God intends us to, but not one Christian lives that book to a tee every day. Romans 3:23 says that we all sin and fall short of the glory of God.

The only reason I am where I am today is because God Almighty used Rachel Hollis's words to be the resounding voice of reason I needed to change.

Despite having swallowed that book whole in a matter of days, I was still smoking pot and drinking, but I had an increased self-awareness to start making some changes to step into the life I wanted to live. The life I knew I was called to live. The life God put me here to live.

On the heel of her book came her podcast, and the practice of daily gratitude and goal setting. An idea molded together by the words of Oprah Winfrey and graphic designer Milton Glaser. I wrote down ten things I was grateful for every day; ten dreams I wanted to make happen, and one goal I would work toward first. The goal was something from the ten dreams or something that would make a number of those dreams a reality faster. I did not do this perfectly each day. In fact, it took a while to get into the habit of documenting ten small things for which to be grateful. I would sometimes break it up into two shifts: 5:00 a.m. and 5:00 p.m. Sometimes, I forgot to jot them down at night. Some days, I forgot altogether. As I worked to make this a habit, something in my mindset shifted. I now had to start looking for things to be grateful for in life. The only rule was they could not be big things. It is easy to be grateful for your home, your health, and your family, when you have them. It is not so easy to be grateful for having piles of laundry to wash, toilets to scrub, and floors to mop. For this, we must get creative. The point is to keep your eye out for small nuggets of gratitude and joy, because when you look for it, you will find it. Take, for example, the color blue. Looking around your space, how many things are blue? Right now in this space as I type, I can count my denim jeans and jacket, my notebook and pen, various stickers on my water bottle, the stripes on my shoes, the pins on my backpack, the siding on my house, the deck where I am seated, and the sky. Fifteen things around me are blue. When you are on the lookout for something, it is easier to find it. The same goes for small things to be grateful for in life.

To this day, I write down that I am grateful for my morning coffee, simply because I *am* so grateful to be able to sip coffee in the wee hours of the morning when no one is around to talk to me. That is the introvert in me. Goal-setting is a very cool thing, and I can attribute it to many changes I have made in my life for the better. The thing is, you write them as if they have happened. Your words must be concise. Remember when I mentioned before that I started writing down that I have not had a drink in a year? That's how concise you must be. Certain things I also wrote down have come true: I do not smoke. I can run five miles without stopping. I am a present mother. I am dependent on Christ, alone. I speak with kindness and edification.

It is a powerful practice because it rewires how your mind speaks to itself. Words are powerful, which we all know. Sticks and stones may break my bones, but words will never hurt me should be a saying that is cast into the lake of fire. Words have the power to build up or tear down. They are weapons and shields. Use them wisely when you are speaking, including when you speak to yourself.

After reading *Girl, Wash Your Face,* and becoming a member of the personal growth club, I still had a lot of work to do when it came to giving up vices that had become addictions and coping mechanisms. I was a work in progress who had a long way to go. Thankfully, it is always about progress, and not perfection, in the self-help club. I had made progress when I attained self-awareness. Leave it to a Cat Stevens song to resonate with this one. The first cut is the deepest when you look at yourself in the mirror and realize you are the problem. I knew I had work to do, that was not even half of the battle. It was, however, the anthem of my new-found motivation. The *star-spangled banner* over my head. I had work to do, and I feared what I would have to let go, in order to get to where I wanted to be. I was also scared of what would happen to my life if I stayed in the state of stuck I was in. The latter outweighed the former.

You know how they say that you cannot heal in the place that made you sick? That is capital 'T' truth. At least it was for me. It wasn't until we sold our house in Dublin, Ohio and packed up and moved to the Poconos, that I was able to get completely sober. Even in my mess back in Ohio, I had felt the Lord lay on my heart that we were to leave Dublin. At first, I did not know where. He did not reveal that to me until later. I told my husband I was feeling like the Papa, God, was calling us into ministry somewhere other than where we were. It seemed like a crazy thing. Was I so much on drugs that I felt like God was calling me out of Ohio? Did I really dislike Ohio so much that I just wanted out, and was looking for a way? I wasn't sure. So, we prayed. And we prayed, and prayed, and prayed. I was starting to ease up on the pot enough that I felt like God was speaking to me, and I wasn't just stoned out of my gourd. I remember we were sitting in the den in our old house and out of my mouth came, "What about the Poconos?" What? Where were the Poconos? I had heard of that area before. I thought it was maybe a beach resort. *Dear God, please let it be a beach resort.* Spoiler alert: it is *not* a beach resort. It is in the northeast mountains of Pennsylvania, where it snows, *a lot.* It is also cold, *a lot.* We did some research on the area, and that is how I found out, to my heart's sadness, that it was not near the beach. Or any beach. Long Island is, perhaps, the closest beach, which is almost two hours away from the Poconos.

After much researching, my husband and I agreed that it was something we needed to really be praying about. Our prayers were confirmed, both on the side of wisdom and clarity, and discernment in what the Lord wanted from us and where He wanted to take us.

God can use anyone and anything to speak to you. Our prayers were confirmed in an episode of *Law and Order: SVU,* of all things. The victim in the episode was murdered in New York City, but the investigation led them to... *the Poconos.*

As if we needed any more confirmation, when we started the real estate selling and buying process, things could not have fallen into place more perfectly. We put our house on the market and had showings scheduled for when we would venture to Pennsylvania to house hunt ourselves. Just when my hope was starting to dwindle of us finding a home to call our own in a place loaded with houses that were only used as vacation getaways, we walked into the final house on our third attempt and felt immediately at home. Not only was the layout like our current home, it felt like it was where we were supposed to be all along. It took three weekend journeys, and countless hours in the car to find this space. And just when my patience with this whole process was starting to run thin, God showed us where he wanted us, just in the nick of time. In June of 2019, we began paperwork proceedings. The following week, we entered the closing phase on our home in Dublin. Immediately after entering into contract with a buyer, we put an offer on the house in Pennsylvania, and it was accepted. We sold our Ohio home five days before closing on our new one. God's perfect timing. Not only had our prayers been confirmed— and answered— they were answered in such a perfectly timed way, that it was only God who could have made it all happen.

Fast forward a few months to August 2019, as we continued to put the finishing touches on our new home to make it ours. My drinking and smoking were getting out of hand. I knew the Lord was nudging at my spirit to lay things entangling me in sin aside, i.e. drinking, smoking like a freight train. I also knew that I was ready to start doing the legwork to get to where I knew I needed, desired, and was called to be. I had been feeling the tug on my heart strings for a while to let these things go. I also knew that there were so many unknowns that came with living a life of sobriety and surrender, that I was still feeling a bit timid. I knew that if I did not get a handle on my drinking, it would get worse, and I also knew that being a non-smoker was a box I had always wanted to check since I picked up my first cigarette at nineteen years old.

I was cognizant that I could not give up drinking without giving up smoking. I also knew that I was not ready to give up the pot. I started taking some steps to cut out some things without feeling like I had to give it all up at once. The thought of giving up too many vices at once was scary, and the reality of living a life where I did not have any coping mechanisms outside of prayer was a life I had never lived before. Even when I first came to Christ as a young twenty-something, I still drank on the weekends and smoked cigarettes. The thought about how much I would be giving up at once, without having much to replace it with, was paralyzing. I knew Jesus was enough, but I had doubts about my own capabilities.

On August 1, 2019, I drank my last drink and embarked upon my venture of going a whole year without a drink. The following week, I smoked my last cigarette as a smoker. Anyone who identifies as a drinking smoker will tell you that drinking and smoking go together. They are like two peas in a pod for a lot of us. Not everyone who is a smoker is a drinker, and not everyone who is a drinker is a smoker. But many drinkers also smoke and will smoke more while they are drinking. For me, they went together, but I also knew that I could smoke without drinking. That addiction was stronger for me. It still is. I knew myself well enough to know that if I was going to give up drinking, I had to have it all out of the house. I could not have any stock in my refrigerator without being tempted to drink.

The one thing that made me feel empowered enough to start on the road to becoming a non-smoker who did not drink, was my daily journaling.. I wrote in my journal for a whole year that I did not smoke, until I actually gave it up. I had been writing that I was not a smoker, even though I actually was, because I knew that rewiring my brain was going to be crucial. Anyone who has an addiction to nicotine will tell you that when they attempt to quit, they hope that they can make it through the first three days, or that they hope to fight the urge to buy a pack. John Maxwell says that hope is not a strategy, and that is so true. Hope is not a strategy when you need a plan. The plan was to rethink how I thought about being a smoker. I did not want to *hope* that I could get through the first few days of nicotine withdrawals without caving, I wanted to *know* that I could because *I am not a smoker.* I knew that if I wanted to hold myself to a higher standard of accountability, I had to talk differently to myself about it. For me, *I am not a smoker* is something I wanted to identify as, and *I haven't had a drink in a year* was a goal I wanted to achieve. In order to do those, I had to rewire my brain. It is incredible how powerful words are. They can build up, tear down, and create new things. Incredible.

By that December, I was starting to approach the moment in my personal growth journey when stepping away from the bong became necessary. I knew that it was becoming a hindrance to my personal growth, ministry, and marriage. It was the one thing I did not want to let go of, while also being the one thing I knew I needed to quit. I knew that it was getting to where it was going to ruin everything, I had worked so hard to achieve and prayed so hard to change. Like a Christina Aguilera song, I kept going right back to the one thing I needed to walk away from. It would end up destroying my marriage and the life we were building together in Christ if I did not lay it aside.

New Year's Eve of 2019, I smoked the last of the marijuana I had. I cannot sit here and say I never looked back. I still look back. I still want to smoke and feel that high. However, I know that I cannot return to that part of my life if I am going to continue the path to glory and holiness in the Lord, for His purpose and ministry. It is hard. Some days, I cry over how much time in my life I lost to the cloud of smoke while simultaneously grieving the stoner life I had when I used to feel like I could escape. But that does not serve me, my marriage, or my growth. You cannot pour old wine into a new wineskin. It will not hold.

What could have been used by the devil to destroy my life and marriage, God turned into good, and helped us rebuild and become stronger. Our marriage and lives are better than they have ever been before. When people say that there is nothing better than walking in God's Will, they are right. I have been all levels of high, and this one is my favorite. It is hard at times, but it is always good.

Things that helped me:

1. **I knew I had to think differently about the life I was about to step into.** I could not allow myself to be afraid of the life I was ready and eager to step into, and still cling to what I knew I needed to let go. I started writing down that I was not someone who smoked, to prepare my mindset for when the time came to lay the Marlboros aside. I decided that it had to be a goal and an identity I wanted to achieve, so that it could stop being a crutch to lean on. I needed Jesus to be my crutch, and to have the confidence of knowing I could get through hard things, without running to something to help me escape or numb. I needed to tell myself that, not only was I not a smoker who had also gone a year without a sip of alcohol, but that I was also dependent on Christ, alone, to get me through hard things. I knew that if I was going to lay aside every sin that kept me from the life I was put here to live, that I had to start talking to myself differently about it, and not bring about self-defeating thoughts. I needed to have confidence in my own tenacity, and confidence in my Savior, that I could do this.

2. **Prayer and the art of perseverance.** When I was going through nicotine withdrawals, I did not get a wink of sleep for 21 days. For 21 days, I did not eat or sleep and only had the sustenance of coffee

and Jesus to get me through the days of mommy-ing and wifey-ing. I kept telling myself that *I am not a smoker,* that *I can do all things through Christ who strengthens me* (Phil. 4:13), and that *His Grace is sufficient for me, because His power is made perfect in my weakness* (2 Cor. 12:9). Those famous Scriptures, along with my power statement I had been writing for a year, were the tools I had in my toolbox on the top shelf, readily available to me when I needed to pull one out and use it. I cried, lashed out, and felt powerless so often, yet in those moments, I extended grace to myself, received grace from my family, and prayed to find the strength I needed.

Friends are not Forever

Back in 2015, I had been working at a retailer for campers and camping equipment in London, Ohio as a retail associate, and later a receptionist for the service and sales departments. Within the first few months there, I became close friends with Rachel*, a woman I knew from the area.

It is a *ridiculously small* farming town where everyone knew everyone or was related to someone who knew everyone, including their personal business.

We became exceedingly close friends during our time working together. I even started going to her church's Bible study nights on Wednesdays. I became intertwined with her family and some of her friends. I immediately felt like I was part of the gang. They were all welcoming and invited me into their quaint and precious tribe. It was bliss.

We went through all the things best friends went through: boyfriends, heartache, moving into new apartments, swimming and lunches, inside jokes, and catching up over glasses of wine and too many cigarettes. And because we were work friends on top of real-life besties, she was my person at work, too. My days at work were gloomy when she was not there because, well, she was my work person.

Like most new friendships, there are other friends of that new friend you also meet. At the beginning of our friendship, everything was peachy-keen, and there was so much fun, connection, and new discoveries. As our new friendship grew, things started to become peachy only on the surface. The ugly pit reared its face as time started to move along.

I want to preface this by saying that this is my account of how things appeared to me. By no means do I wish to mislead or to misconstrue anything that may not be true. This is how things "went down", from my perspective, as it pertains to Rachel and Pam*.

As our friendship moved along, there was one character of this story that played a role that is hurtful to process. Pam was Rachel's long-time, and still current, best friend. She seemed like she genuinely wanted to be my friend, as well. Then, the tide turned. I started to notice that conversations I had with Pam, would be misrepresented to our mutual friend, Rachel. This naturally brought about confusion and division.

One conversation in particular, was misrepresented to such degree that Rachel barely talked to me at work that day until I was able to open up some lines of communication.

To this day, I do not remember all of the things that were said between Pam and I in this exchange, but I remember enough to know that I was invited to lunch, so we could talk *church shop* and try to build a more solid foundation between the two of us as Rachel's close friends. Little did I know that Pam and Rachel had had a disagreement and were trying to patch things up, so that conversation got misrepresented in a way that made it seem like we were meeting behind Rachel's back to talk smack.

No wonder Rachel did not want to talk to me that day. She thought I was plotting behind her back, which was not the case. It seemed to me that Pam was threatened by my friendship with Rachel and wanted to start trouble. This may or may not be the case, but that is how it appeared to me, and still seems to this day.

I was able to squash that in Rachel's mind by explaining my side of things and showing her our conversation, which happened via text message. Texting is a blessing and a curse. It is a great way to stay connected when you cannot talk on the phone for whatever reason but is also a great way to allow for misreading and misunderstanding. Text does not inflect tone of voice, leaving a lot open for interpretation as it filters through their perception and reception of what is being said.

I knew from then on that I had to tread lightly when it came to conversations with Pam, and I immediately cancelled our lunch plans. I did not know her agenda, so to protect myself and my friendship with Rachel, I knew I could not allow myself to get tangled in the web of deceit and lies.

To my face, Pam was a completely different person than how she was behind my back. That, my precious reader, is not someone who should be in your community. When respect is no longer being served, leave the table.

Time moved us along, and Rachel and I were still connected at the hip inside and outside of work. I still went to Wednesday night Bible study, I still attended church gatherings, and I still showed up to Sunday service.

Some months later, I met my new boyfriend, who is now my husband, and Rachel was in a new relationship with a guy from work. I remember her telling me on various occasions, before dating this guy, that she was going to be picky about the man she wanted to pursue for a relationship. We were both looking for long-lasting relationships with Godly men who would lead to marriage and happily ever after. To be honest, with no bias, my guy was exactly that, while hers was still struggling to figure out what he believed when it came to God and faith. I remember giving her some warning while they were in the early phases of dating. I reminded her to tread lightly, to take things slowly, and pray to let God make a decent man out of him.

I know that when I was blinded by love, advice like that went in one ear and out the other. Rachel was the same way. We are very much the kind of women who are going to do what we are going to do, and it is not going to matter what anyone says. Jesus, Himself, would have to be the one to tell us the hard truths for us to start considering such hard realities.

Especially when we think the man we seek is cute and is starting to "court" us, by flirting and bringing us delicious coffee in the morning.

Amid the changes in our personal lives, things were shifting at work, within the company. Hours were being cut, and new employees were being hired. Which did not make any sense to me at the time, until I began to realize that I was being phased out. As a single mom, I could not afford to live off the few hours I was being scheduled, so I found another job very quickly. I put in my two weeks and left with a heavy heart. I loved the people I worked with and the friendships I had made there. I did not love the company. I felt jaded and shafted, hence, my parting was bittersweet. Even though I was excited for the new employment opportunity, I knew that I would miss my co-workers dearly. I had grown fond of many of them, especially the sales team and my fellow receptionist.

Rachel and I remained close and still communicated regularly. I remember being in fervent prayer for her and her new boyfriend, who, to be quite frank, was leading her a lot closer to sin than to Jesus, all while she was trying to bring him to the Lord and redemption.

I do not know if you have ever seen the visual of one person standing on a chair or table and trying to pull someone up only to be pulled down by the person standing on the ground, but that is what can happen when we try to save someone who does not want to be saved.

In those prayers, the Lord was really laying on my heart to be frank with Rachel and the path she was on, as to warn her to be careful so she did not stray too far from her Savior. I was worried that her new relationship would lead her down a path she would regret if I did not speak up. I was also worried that if I did not bring such hard truths to her attention, that I would end up being disobedient to the nudge of the Holy Spirit to speak with her about such things. I did not want to hurt my friend, but my desire to be obedient to the Spirit was much greater.

I prayed and prayed, and then, I prayed harder. I wanted to speak with love and truth, and bring forth a perspective I felt was being overlooked because of blind lust and love. I sent her a voice message expressing my concern, my love, and my message from the Lord.

I do not remember word for word what I said. I know that I was nervous that it would not be received with love. I know that I was scared for my friend and was aware of the possibility that we would have a disagreement because of it. I now know that I could have worded it all differently. I know that some of the things I said hurt her in ways I cannot imagine. I know that when you are telling someone that the person, they love is not the right one for them, words are so important; not only the ones you choose, but also in how you say them. I know that I could have brought a lot more Jesus and a lot less Hannah when things got heated. I will forever regret that conversation. It was a conversation that shifted our relationship in a terribly negative trajectory. We had fallen out.

In the weeks that followed, I reached out to a few people who knew her well. I remember pleading for their help and their insight, as I nursed my hurt and tried to heal the wounds. Pam told me that she had tried multiple times to speak a similar truth to Rachel, only to learn that it is best to leave things as they are, and let Rachel learn her own lessons. Dear God, how I wish I had known that beforehand.

It is a catch twenty-two. Maybe I would have said it differently. Maybe I would not have said anything at all. I know my prayers would have been different, and just as fervent. I know that I cannot take back the way I said things, no matter how much I wish I could. I know that what is done is done, and even though we mended fences, we will never be what we used to be, regardless of the amount of prayer.

I know that I was doing what God wanted me to do. I know that in hindsight, if we were really the friends I thought we were, we could have reconciled, if it was as important to her as it was to me. She and Pam had reconciled after fights and managed to stay close, but apparently, that was not something we could ever do, because our foundation was different.

In retrospect, God did not want us to be friends for longer than the season we were, because it would have hindered our growth in Him and ourselves. There cannot be true friendship when the importance is categorized differently for both parties. There cannot be long-lasting connection when the foundation is built on sand.

I miss her more than she will ever know. I miss our friendship and the closeness we had. I miss how she used to call me her best friend.

We did reconcile for the sake of forgiveness and tried to move forward, not necessarily as friends, even though I tried to get things back. We just were not meant to be forever friends, and that is okay. It hurts, but it is okay.

She ended up marrying her guy, and I married mine. We were not a part of each other's weddings, as we had once dreamed.

I am still married. She is not. She later filed for divorce after realizing all the things I tried to tell her. Shit happens.

After I had moved to Dublin to start my life with my new husband, I attended a luncheon at her church. The invite was sent to me from a family member of Rachel's who was trying to help mend the hurt.

God bless that woman, so much. Her kindness is genuine and her heart so tender.

I went and was seated at a table with some friendly and familiar faces. A few of them I stay in contact with to this day, thanks to Facebook and technology and a shared love of *Scandal*. It was a beautiful time, and the food was divine. Rachel was unable to attend, due to work.

Pam actually was there. We shared small talk a bit, and when I asked how Rachel was doing, Pam showed her true colors in the gossip which then took place. I stayed quiet and just thought to myself how grateful I was to no longer be in connection with someone who gossips behind my back. She twisted my own words at one point in an attempt to bring division between Rachel and me, for whatever reason. At least I had the stones to say things to Rachel's face.

I left the luncheon grateful to connect with old pals who cared about me, regardless of what happened with Rachel. I also left with opened eyes and new perspective on why things were the way they were.

God is good. All the time.

Things that helped me:

1. **I had to let go of expectations.** I could not sit and wonder all the days of my life how unfair it seemed that I lost a friend because I was honest. I could not sit and stew in the hurt that I had from that loss, or I would never be able to move on in life. I had to let go of what was because it simply could never be. I will never get my friend back. It pains me more than words can express how much I wish I could. Even though I know it is not what God had planned, that does not make the hurt less painful, nor the reality that I was not as important to her as she was to me, any less bearable. It hurts. It sucks. I wish this chapter in my life had a different ending. But I cannot wish on a thousand stars for something to be different when the Creator of those stars had a different plan.

2. **Reconciliation does not always bring forth healing.** Just because we reconciled and apologized for things that were said and done, did not mean that we were able to return to how it was. Reconciliation does not always mean healing, even though it brings forgiveness. Forgiveness does not always bring forth reconciliation outside of being able to move forward. Some wounds must close on their own with time, and that does not always mean they will be healed. Some scars never heal beyond the tissue. They stay at surface level and serve as a reminder of how to be a friend and provide a lesson to be learned. I do not know if I will ever be healed before Christ calls me home. I think that I will always be wounded, guarded, and careful about who I call "friend". Maybe that is all there is to take from this: life lessons, relationship lessons, and the wonder of how beautiful and precious it would have been to have her in my wedding photos.

3. **Let it go.** I have yet to do this. It is safe to say that I still have a lot of hurt. I still grieve her and what we shared. It is safe to say that sometimes, life sucks and we will not always have the answers as to why things happen the way they do— answers we like, anyway. It is also safe to say that I have yet to fully let things go because I still wonder, dream, and pray about her often. I still have healing to do. It has been five years, and the wounds do not feel as raw as they did, but when that scar tissue gets snagged, it is like salt from my tears seeps in and makes it fresh all over again. I am still working on being like Elsa and letting it go. We will make it, sweet reader. We will make it.

CHAPTER 11

Paper Rings

My husband and I met online. I know it is seemingly the norm to hear that from couples nowadays, but at the time, it was still a little taboo. It was happening in real time to thousands of couples, but there was still a side glance that came from folks who would hear that was how you met your significant other.

I reached out first. I was never shy when it came to reaching out to someone I was interested in— when it came to the Internet, anyway. Face-to-face, forget it. I was timid and hesitant every time. Being tucked safely behind a keyboard was a different story. The screen was a shield, and each verb, noun, and ampersand could be filtered and considered a few times over before pressing *send*.

When his picture came across my screen on a Christian-based social media app, I did not think twice before trying to slide in his DM's. He was dark, handsome, and had a smile that took my breath away— and still does.

I was not initially looking to meet anyone when I scrolling the feed, although it was an underlying thought when I logged on that maybe the man God had for me was in the places I was not willing to consider, due to previous bad experiences (i.e. I had met my rapist online).

Then, I saw him. His cute smile and his dark skin that had a glow. I saw him, and I knew I wanted to talk to him. What is it that Shania says, "Love gets me every time"?

I sent him a message, and to my surprise, he messaged me back. The formatting of the application was that because it was a Christian community, your profile picture had to be approved before it would be shown on your profile, to ensure it was not provocative or inappropriate. I had the standard grey background with a white silhouette female as my profile picture, and he messaged back.

Spoiler alert: I found out a couple of weeks ago that because he is in the tech field, he searched my name and city and found my Facebook profile. Ha. Of course he did.

We exchanged messages for a few days, and after some time, he asked me for my phone number. We spent our first phone conversation talking about God, Jesus, and the Bible. For five hours. Five. Hours. I had never had such a lengthy, in-depth conversation with someone who was still a borderline stranger.

I remember when I first saw him in person. We had been talking on the phone for a few weeks, and we decided the best place for us to meet was church. At the time, he was church shopping, because he had just stepped down as an associate pastor, due to conflict with the head pastor. The head pastor was having an affair. When my husband, Lenin, confronted him and brought forth Scripture to back up his argument as to why the pastor should step down, he refused. He wanted to have his cake and eat it, too. My husband could not serve under a pastor who was operating his church in that manner. So, Lenin left.

He agreed to come to my church to check it out, and I remember being all school-girl giddy to meet him in person. I told my friend, who was later my matron-of-honor, to "let me know what she thought of him". Fellas, that is Girl Code for let me know if you think he is cute and worth my time.

She approved.

He was *ridiculously cute* and also had an interesting conversation with one of our pastors, which had me floored. Guys, one of the hottest things to do in front of a church girl is to quote Scripture and flex your Bible knowledge.

It was a glorious Sunday.

Not long after that, we had our first date. Dinner, coffee at a local coffee shop, and a movie. It was my definition of perfection. We talked about basically anything and everything. No small talk was needed. For someone who detests small talk because it makes me feel awkward, this gave me life. Also, I want to add that the movie was so boring we both fell asleep. When you can both agree to take a nap because you both think that it was a bad choice of a movie, it is a sign he may be a keeper. This was also after coffee. It was *that* bad.

It also gave me life that my parents also approved of him. They were never too fond of any of the guys I brought home. But they liked him. *Score!*

After a handful of dates and countless hours of conversations and text messages, we started doing a Bible study. Just the two of us. On the Old Testament. God as my witness, I do not care for history. And that was how I viewed that Old Testament. Because that is what it is. LOL.

I met him during a time when I was trying my best to walk as close to Jesus as I could. I was not smoking pot or drinking excessively. I was pretty close to the dictionary definition of a church girl. So, a Bible study with a cute guy I liked and could see myself with for the rest of my life— *sign me up.*

Guys, if there is a girl at your church you fancy, ask her to do a Bible study. That is a great way to find out if she likes you, too.

Now before you go thinking, how *'Little House on the Prairie',* know this: we slept together after talking about the giants of the book of Genesis. Something about learning all these new things was a version of foreplay that I did not know existed. I was attracted to him in a way I had never experienced before.

Do I recommend this? H-E-double hockey sticks *NO.* It is not ideal for Christian couples to do such things that are not of the Lord.

I immediately understood why people say that couples who pray and study the Bible together should do so with other people around, or at least in the actual house of the Lord, not in a living room. Apparently, talking about the exegesis of Genesis is a hot and steamy topic. Church singles, beware.

Did we repent? Yes. Did we regret the slip? Yes. Did we learn from it and wait until we were married? Nope. We are human. Jesus was perfect. It was *good*. Still is.

It led Lenin to such conviction that he stepped down from seeking a pastor role anywhere until he felt he was made right with God. He could not, in his mind, speak behind a pulpit again until he sat in the pews and made things right with his Savior.

Some old woman in Texas just fainted at the thought of pre-marital fornication. It is okay, Betty. We are living in holy matrimony now.

I want to address something you may be thinking. Yes, I called out and lost a friend for sleeping with her boyfriend. He was not in the church with her. She was hoping to lead him to Christ. My guy was already there. It is vastly different to slip into sin with someone who already knows Jesus, than to jump the bones of someone you are trying to lead to Christ. It taints your testimony if they are not a believer. I am not saying that either one of us was right. I am saying it is different.

Lenin and I were equally yoked.[1] Still are. Am I using Scripture to justify it? No. There is a difference between justifying and explaining. Also let us not get it twisted that I am not defending what we did. You, dear reader, may be in a season of your life where you have slipped or are thinking about it because, let us be honest, church guys who know their Bible are a level of hot that Adam Levine will never be. No offense, Adam. I only want you to understand that there is a difference between trying to be with someone you think you could lead to Jesus who does not already know him and, being with someone who already does. No one gets to Heaven on someone else's salvation. And it is much harder to witness to someone if you are living in sin.

We are not called to perfection. Although I know Scripture says to be more like Christ[2], He was perfect, and we are not. Notice that Scripture says to be *like,* as in trying to do what is right. Notice it is also written that we fall short[3].

We are called to repentance and to live rightly with God. Huge difference. That does not give us a free pass to sin and be led into temptation[4]. It affords us grace, guidance, and mercy when our hearts are being convicted to change and do what God instructs us to do. Notice I said 'convicted', not 'condemned'. There is a difference there, as well. One is from the devil, himself, and the other is a correction from the Holy Spirit.

The best way I can describe them is that conviction is a tug on your heartstrings to change your behavior and pray. Condemnation is a sick feeling in the pit of your stomach that makes you want to throw up and hide from God. That is where the devil can try to ensnare you and lead you away from Christ. Condemnation makes you feel bad for not doing the right thing. It leaves you wanting to blame yourself and hide in a dark hole, or under the covers. Conviction is knowing in your spirit you that need to talk to Jesus about it. There is a nudge. Condemnation will make you feel like you cannot tell anyone, especially Jesus. That nasty devil is a trickster, do not fall in his trap. The best way to discern when you feel you cannot tell a difference in how you are feeling, is to ask God to take it away if it is not from Him. This does a couple of things.   It shines a light on how you are feeling, to help you discern what to do next. It also opens a line of communication to talk to God about what is going on, whether you feel the need to ask for forgiveness or not. He will lead you.

It is also written that there is no condemnation for those who are in Christ[5]. That is capital "T" truth. But do not be misled. Satan, himself, tempted Jesus in the garden for forty days and nights, citing Scripture to Him in an attempt to get Jesus to slip and fall[6]. Please do not think he will not have the audacity to do the same to you, and use the Word of God against you. Therefore, we must always pray for the discernment of the things we are feeling, as to not be led astray by a slippery serpent who will stop at nothing to make you slip.

The target on my back just got bigger for calling out his games to the masses. That is okay with me. It simply means I am doing my job.

The times Lenin and I slipped into sin were few and far between after that first experience. We did not go at it like jack rabbits. We knew it was wrong, so we tried our best to not intentionally climb the ladder to the slippery slope. But it still happened, occasionally. Each time after, we always prayed together, as well as individually.

Months went by, and things just keep getting better and better. I knew from the time I hung up the phone during our very first phone conversation that he was the one I wanted to be with for the rest of my life. Somehow, I just knew. I never *knew* like that before. All the previous guys I had dated up until then were guys I either *thought* I could be with forever or *knew* it was only for a season. With him, I knew. I knew like I know every *NSYNC and Britney Spears song as soon as the first beat drops. I knew like I knew the backroads of Hilliard, and like how I knew every word of my favorite Bible verses. I knew.

You know how they say, "When you know, you know?" It is the absolute, God's-honest truth. I knew.

We had our first date November 4, 2016, were engaged by mid-January, and were married on June 10, 2017. Apparently, he knew, too. I am writing these words on our three-year anniversary. We are on the last leg of a quarantine and have been "sheltering in place" for weeks. Yeah, you read that part right.

One week before we were to be married, I started moving things into his house in Dublin, Ohio. I knew that when we got back from our honeymoon in Punta Cana, Dominican Republic (his birthplace) that the last thing I would want to do is move boxes and unpack more clothes than what left with me to globe-trot with my new husband. We even repainted and set up our son's room. One of my favorite memories after we were married was stepping foot into "our home" after the reception and opening the cards and gifts from our generous and thoughtful friends and family, while I ate a huge burrito bowl from Chipotle. The bride never really eats at the reception. I did get a few bites of the delicious salmon, but I was also busy talking to people, and I had to be mindful of how much I was eating, because the corset top of my gown was not forgiving in the least. No room for a food-filled belly for this bride.

Our honeymoon was grandiose. It was beautiful and momentous, and I had one too many cosmopolitans in the pool with the swim-up bar. It was all-inclusive, so I took full advantage. We watched the sunrise on the beach every morning and walked along the shoreline every sunset. I even bought some pot from a Jamaican one night on the beach. Full disclosure: I had drunk to the point of sickness, that in my *previous stoner life* opinion, cannabis was going to be the only thing to remedy it. It helped. In fact, it cured it, and I did not even wake with a hangover. Cheers to you, Rastafarian acquaintance. I hold you dear in my heart and the memory of you teaching a newly married couple how to roll a joint on the beach. Ah, vacation. The justification for all things not of Jesus.

We returned from our honeymoon a few shades darker than when we left, and I personally had an aching heart from sheer longing of sunrises over the Caribbean, authentic Dominican beer, and toes in the sand, like a Zac Brown Band song. Also, the unknown return date to the beaches of the DR was the topic of daily discussion. I even joked about having our child air-lifted and parachuted to us while in the water. I hear the beaches of Punta Cana are some of the best in the world. I am happy that my bar is now set to impossible standards of what a beach should look like. Not only should they be crystal clear and saltier than a pretzel, let us hope they also have cigar dealers with more to sell under the surface of the humidor walking the shores for way too drunk new brides who thinks *Gone In 60 Seconds* is more than a movie, but also a drinking game.

My husband is my true best friend. He is not only my go-to for Bible verse citations and the "you won't believe what I just saw" tidbits of social media life. He also is the mirror I look into for when I need to do better, keep going, or change my outlook altogether. He does not complete me. He does not make me whole. But he does give me that sense of "it is not that I *can't* live without you, it is that I don't *want* to live without you" vibe. He is good. He was worth the wait. He was worth all the failed relationships and broken hearts and sad Taylor Swift songs. He is one of the few people I refuse to do life without. For better or worse.

We have had our fair share of hard times in the short period we have been married. Disagreements and laughs. Hard conversations and talks about the future full of promise. Actual fights and walking away for a bit to cool off before continuing to hash things out. We have been through a lot; we have also overcome it all.

It all has made us stronger, better, and more in sync. It has brought us closer and breathed forgiveness and grace when it could have led us to give up or crumble.

I ended up becoming addicted to marijuana. That addiction nearly destroyed our marriage. Not only were we struggling financially for it, so was our relationship. I was feeling things like shame, burden, helplessness, hopelessness A few months after we moved to Pennsylvania I was struggling with self-medication and, like I was not being seen or desired by him in the ways I needed. The list could go on and on. When I was open with him about the things I was dealing with, it was hurtful for the both of us. I shared things I did not want to share. I was open and transparent and tried to be as vulnerable as possible, even though

I knew what I would say would be hurtful. I also knew that if I kept it to myself it would hurt our marriage more in the end.

What is hidden cannot be healed.[7]

I do not know who needs this, but, dear one, you are not a mistake just because you made one. You are worthy of the love you crave and the attention you seek from the man you love and with whom you exchanged vows. You are not someone to be ashamed of just because you did something shameful. You will get through this. I promise.

I hope that was just as much for someone else as it was for me. I know I needed those words, personally.

Here is the thing: marriage is—all caps— 'WORK.' It is hard, but it is worth it. None of it is easy all the time. There were times when I was so depressed and lost in piles of laundry and was being suffocated by Lysol toilet cleaner on a weekly basis. That was not a reflection of my marriage; it was a reflection of me being unaware how to work on myself while in a marriage. My husband has always been good. He has always been faithful, willing to listen, and understanding of my point of view, even if it does not immediately align with his.

We have always had to work at this. It does not make it easier when we ignore the issues and fail to speak the truth. It does not make it harder when we are mid-disagreement and trying to work through whatever the "'it" is. But it always makes it worth it. Disney messed us up in so many ways. You do not always meet the right guy when you have run away from home and washed up somewhere. Sometimes, we have to kiss a few frogs and let things go before we can have the *happily ever after*. The happily ever after does not come after the wedding as you ride off into the sunset in a horse-drawn carriage. The *happily ever after* happens after you have had the worst fight, or said the meanest things, and still can go to bed holding each other and saying, "I love you". The *happily ever after* comes when you are drowning in the worst of life, and you make it through to the better, together. The *happily ever after* is not a myth, it just does not happen the way Disney princesses might have you to think.

If you are in your happily ever after, and it is hard right now, there will be better on the other side, if you continue to do the work and have the hard talks. If you are still waiting for your *happily ever after*, know it is out there, but it will take work to keep it.

Know that you cannot go into any kind of relationship looking for your other half. If you think you need another half, I challenge you to do the work for you to be whole. Marriage is not 50/50. It is two whole people coming together and putting in 100 percent of their effort to make it work. Some days, you cannot put in all that you normally have, because it seems too much. Thankfully, on those days, your partner should be coming in with extra effort and making up the difference to make it 100 percent. That may take the role of cleaning the house, folding laundry, or taking turns with dinner and homework. Maybe it is one of you ordering takeout while the other one picks it up, or eating off paper plates, so you have less dishes to do. There will be days when you must realize you need some help, for the sake of taking some time to recharge and refuel. There is no shame in that. Asking for help to bring in the groceries or wash the dishes is not something you should feel guilt over. They eat the food, too, sis. They use plates, and cups, and forks, too.

Especially if you work outside of the house, do not be led by the societal norms and stigmas that women must do all the housework and all the grocery shopping. It is okay to send your husband to the store with a list and Google images of which tampons to buy you.

Husbands, I guarantee nothing will get you luckier than your wife seeing you walking around with a mop or a toilet scrubber.

It has been said, *'give her a house, and she will give you a home'*. Help her, if she asks. In fact, ask her if she needs help before she is ready to rip off the heads of your children and punch you in the face for not replacing the toilet paper roll. I hope you read that with the sarcasm I intended. In case you did not, she is not going to rip off any heads or punch anyone in real life. That may look like tears falling into the sink and muffled f bombs while she waits for the freshly mopped floors to dry.

I am blessed to have a husband who is not afraid to scrub toilets, do the dishes, or ask if he can help fold the laundry. I am blessed that he is not ashamed to be seen in the tampon aisle alone. I am blessed that we can share in the housework when he notices I am overwhelmed or burned-out. I am blessed that we have made it this far, and overcome as much as we have. It is only with honest communication, hard conversations, extra doses of grace and forgiveness, and oodles of prayer that we are where we are. To God be the glory.

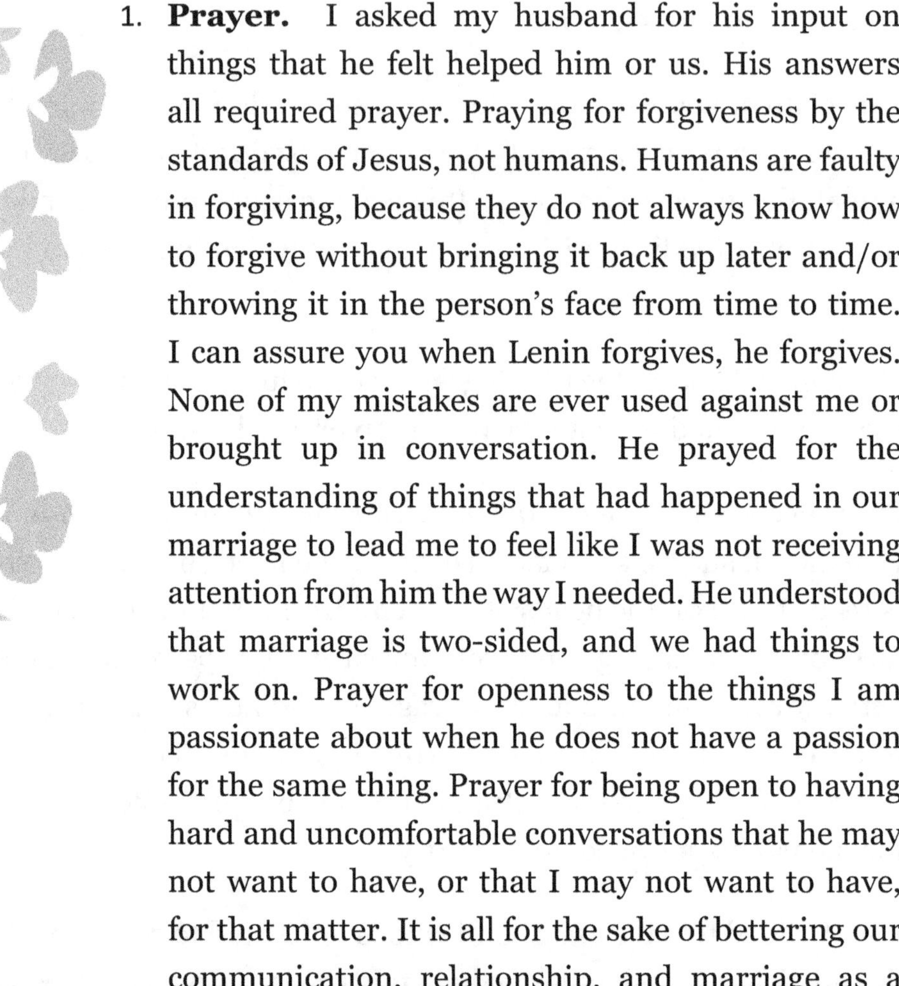

1. **Prayer.** I asked my husband for his input on things that he felt helped him or us. His answers all required prayer. Praying for forgiveness by the standards of Jesus, not humans. Humans are faulty in forgiving, because they do not always know how to forgive without bringing it back up later and/or throwing it in the person's face from time to time. I can assure you when Lenin forgives, he forgives. None of my mistakes are ever used against me or brought up in conversation. He prayed for the understanding of things that had happened in our marriage to lead me to feel like I was not receiving attention from him the way I needed. He understood that marriage is two-sided, and we had things to work on. Prayer for openness to the things I am passionate about when he does not have a passion for the same thing. Prayer for being open to having hard and uncomfortable conversations that he may not want to have, or that I may not want to have, for that matter. It is all for the sake of bettering our communication, relationship, and marriage as a whole. Learning how to lean into extending grace the way Jesus does.

2. **Learning each other's love language.** The way we give and receive love are different as individuals. Meaning that the love language couples speak will be different, as well. A great resource to understanding

your own love language is a book by Gary Chapman called *The Five Love Languages*. While we have a couple of mutual love languages, like words of affirmation and quality time, they also differ with me really speaking the language of receiving gifts and him really speaking the language of acts of service. Learning the love language your partner speaks will not only improve your communication and facilitate meaningful connection, it will also improve your intimacy.

3. **Collectively engaging in or abstaining from specific practices.** Praying together and engaging in a couple's devotion, or reading a book on marriage with discussion topics helps open lines of communication and redirect the focus of your marriage to Christ. Carve out time to spend without kids. Make it happen. If you cannot find a sitter, make a lunch date while the kids are at school and the little one is napping. If you can find a sitter, go to dinner, go to breakfast, grab coffee, and drink it at the coffee shop. Carve out time to spend with each other away from regular everyday responsibilities of work and home life. Guys, flirt with her, court her. Ladies, get dressed up a little bit. It is nice to remind yourself you are more than a laundry troll with spit up on your shirt. If you do not have kids, great! Lean into that freedom and schedule a weekly date night around work schedules. Make your partner a priority. Also, I am not going to sit here and preach to you about remaining abstinent from sex in the 21st century, let us be realistic. So, I say this, if you think, or know, that the person you are with is the person you are going to be with for the rest of your life, just wait. It is worth it not wondering if they are going to text you back or call you the day

after. When you are married, you get to wake up next to them the next morning and have no wonders on whether they are going to stick around or not. To be frank, divorce is messy and expensive. Besides, married people have the most fulfilling sex ever. I have had all the sex— pre-marital as well as within the confines of marriage—, and it is worth noting that sex with my husband is the best I have ever had on multiple levels. If you are in the church, you know what the Bible says about this topic. I plead with you, do not risk stepping into sin for the sake of an orgasm. It is never worth it, even if you end up marrying them. Just don't do it.

She Will Be Loved

Goal weight is a myth.

This is a revelation that came to me on day two of a three-day women's conference I attended. It is a gut-punching, breath-taking revelation which took me years of self-hatred and comparison to realize. The idea that "you will feel good about yourself if you reach a certain number on the scale" is completely bogus. I was a size zero and still found myself living in a past body, from when I was much heavier. I still live in a past body at times. I have gained about fifteen pounds, and lost five, since going into quarantine in the middle of March 2020, and I am still trying to not mentally beat myself up for snacking too much, or not portioning out the ice cream according to the label, because my favorite jeans are slightly snug. I hit my desired pant size and number on a scale, and yet I still compare myself to others.

I used to be about 60 pounds heavier than I am at the moment. My journey with health and weight is one that is not uncommon. Unfortunately, it is also non-stop. I used to abuse my body in ways I still regret to this day. I took laxatives, starved myself, and then

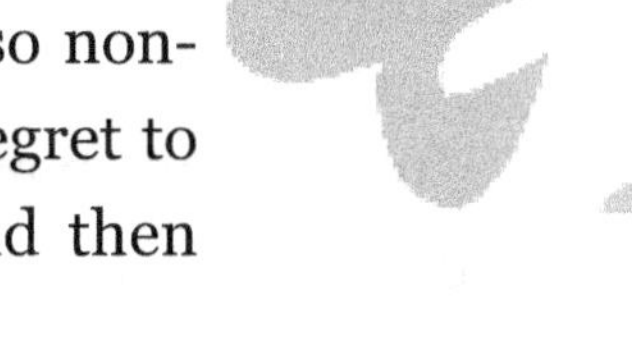

went to the gym to punish my body for the one meal I did eat. As a young adult, I used to binge eat late at night, while everyone else was asleep, to hide the addiction I had to food. I hid food in my room and hoarded it like a squirrel gathering nuts for the winter.

When I met my husband, I was just starting to come out of my laxative abuse and was an unhealthy level of skinny. I remember my dad mentioning, one summer, that he could see my ribs and he thought I was too thin, I thought my weight was perfect, even though I still hated that I *skin rolls* when I sat down. Skin rolls. When overweight people think that super skinny people do not have a body image problem, I want to smack them in the face or punch them in the throat.

Since this is not of the Lord, I will settle for having a conversation over coffee about this taboo topic of body image and shame.

A few months before we were married, I developed bad habits of eating more than what I was working off, at my desk job. I packed on more pounds than I ever had carried around on my body, in a few short months, simply because of bad habits. I was eating more calories than I was burning off with the lack of exercise in my life. The vending machine at work and drive-thru fast food places at lunch became daily staples that were held together with diet soda and energy drinks loaded with sugar. Not to mention all the sugar-filled mints that were kept at my desk for the sales staff and guests that I ate like a meal— before and after actually eating a meal.

After we got married, the weight kept piling on when I slipped into a depression, fueled by emotional eating and alcohol. I went from being merely skin and bones to— as my then 8-year-old son put it plainly— looking like I was pregnant.

Those were his words when he got off the bus one day. It broke my heart, while also motivating me to make a change.

That was the catalyst I needed to get my weight under control. I signed up for Weight Watchers and started exercising. I tracked what I ate, joined the 5 a.m. club at the gym, and worked hard at losing the weight I packed on after meeting my husband and "letting myself go".

It was emotionally and physically hard work getting down to my "goal weight". I felt triumphant during the weeks I lost pounds, and defeated when my weight stayed the same or increased.

When I went from an XL to an S/M in tops I was elated, but I still hated the way I looked. I was terrified of gaining it back and was still looking at my stomach in the mirror like it was a constant threat to return to how big it used to be. I still do this every day. I look at the profile of my body in the mirror, just to check. If you are also still living in a past body, you are not alone, my friend. I may have ditched the diet soda and energy drinks, but one habit remained the same: checking myself in the mirror every day to see if I was looking any slimmer or trimmer than the day before. I still have a problem with how I view myself in the mirror without clothes, to cover things up, or use makeup to conceal my dark circles and crow's feet. Self-hatred of your body knows no boundaries.

I have been both overweight with body image issues and skinny with body image issues. The one thing that remained the same was how I viewed myself in the mirror, regardless of what the scale said, or what size pant I was putting on. And spare me the elastic waistband jokes. No waistband is comfortable when you feel like garbage about the way you look. Let us stop validating unhealthy lifestyles and body images by saying leggings and oversized t-shirts are the saving grace we all need. "Gag me with ruffage", as Kevin McAlister said.

No amount of elastic or oversized sweaters will change the way a woman perceives herself when she is buck-naked in front of the mirror. We all grab our fat and wish it went somewhere else. We all look to see if our thighs are touching more or less than they did the day before. We all say the most hateful things to ourselves that we would never dare say to our best friend, simply because we see the beauty in her that she does not see herself. We all point, and pick, and pull, and pray that the unwanted body we are carrying around this world would look like our friends or the body we used to have. We all hate ourselves for blaming our kids for "destroying our bodies". We all secretly wonder if our guy still marvels at us the same now as he did when he first saw us. P.S., he does.

We all wonder where it all went wrong and how to undo what was done. Not one woman who has done any amount of body image work loves the way she looks. Not one. Myself included. It takes years of therapy sessions on a couch and years of daily affirmations to get to where we can see ourselves the way we ought to.

All the things you say to yourself when you are personally attacking the way you look, I say to myself, as well. Why are we so mean to ourselves? Why do we hate the way we look in that pair of jeans, or why can't we be as cute as her with a messy bun and an oversized sweatshirt without looking like a rundown, homeless troll from underneath the bridge on I-70? You know the girl I am talking about. We see her on social media or in the local Walmart and wonder why we cannot look that cute without effort. It is a bitch being a woman at times.

Sure, we love the empowering hashtags and the thought of a community of women empowering women. But that never negates how much we hate the work it takes to be 'Instagrammable'. It is impossible to go to a celebrity's social media feed and not feel threatened. *How is Kate Beckinsale still that fit and trim after thirteen weeks of quarantine? How is Khloé Kardashian turning into a completely different person than the KoKo on the first season of KUWTK?* Let it not go unsaid that I have mad respect for both women. They are beautiful and badass, and I appreciate the beauty they each possess. But do not think that they both love the way they look one hundred percent of the time. I assure you, they do not. Even underneath the hard work and makeup done by a professional, not one verified person on social media loves everything about the way they look all the time.

As women, we fall into the trap of fad diets, comparison, and unhealthy eating habits. We wear clothes that are too big for our bodies to help us grapple with the fact that we do not love ourselves the way we know we should. We have grown up in eras of ever-changing definitions of beauty, and it is hard for us to keep up. One decade it is all about the ThighMaster, spandex, and a crazy obsession with working out. The next decade is centered on hourglass figures and measurements dictated in a Nelly song. It is exhausting. How is a woman to keep up?

It is a trap. And we fall in it every time. How dare we become comfortable in our skin without paying homage to the next trend of thigh gaps and bougie asses? How dare we think that we are beautiful just because our mama told us we were? Magazines, centerfolds and highlight reels on social media tell a different story, and we fall right back into feeling not pretty enough, not skinny enough, and not curvy enough all in the same Instagram scroll.

Somehow, society expects us to be a size zero with a Cardi B butt, perfect skin, the ability to look beautiful without makeup while effortlessly raising children and bringing home half the bacon. I am here for none of it.

Enough is enough, and I call bullshit on the beauty industry.

The expectations on women's appearances is mere hogwash.

I do not even know what you look like, and I can tell you, you are pretty, sexy, and beautiful. The way you laugh makes someone's heart soar. The way you smile lights up the room, and the way your eyes sparkle when you talk about your passion is the most beautiful thing anyone has ever seen.

By the way, your butt looks good, too.

Having been on both sides of the spectrum, I can assure you that no number on a scale defines the way you feel about yourself. Only you have that power. Quit giving it away to images of perfection through filters and makeup and corset tops and Spanx. We must stop putting such pressure on ourselves to be 'her kind of pretty.' You are '*your* kind of pretty.'

If you, too, are tired of the expectations of what the world tells us is beautiful, and want to learn how to look at every angle of yourself in the mirror, then take my hand and let us go galloping into the sunset and leave the rest of the world behind. They can feel like they will never measure up without us. It is time to leave behind the norms we are constantly being pressured to fit into.

There is no right way to look or be. With the ever-changing demands of how beauty is defined from one decade— and one magazine— to the next, let us stop squeezing ourselves into molds we are not meant to fit into.

You are perfectly and wonderfully made[1] just the way you are.

How do we do this? How do we stop telling ourselves we are not enough of any kind? Not pretty, or skinny, or curvy, or fit *enough*.

To be honest with you, I do not have all the answers, but I have some ideas that may help.

These ideas may sound corny. Also, they may seem difficult. They are things I still struggle to do myself at times, but when I force myself to do them, I feel exponentially better about myself than when I do not put them into practice. Telling myself that I do not need an extra scoop of ice cream when I feel in my spirit I *need* that extra scoop of therapy is not acceptable. I am not saying eat the whole tub, but the pint— go for it. Some health guru just died.

May they rest in peace.

Speaking to ourselves in a manner that deprives us of joy is a trait we must learn to let go of. Now obviously, if we are lactose intolerant or get an upset stomach from excessive dairy, let us also remember to proceed with extreme caution. Yet, let us also not deprive ourselves of the joy that comes from the whole cookie Ben & Jerry blessed us with.

It must not go without saying that if you struggle with binge eating —seek help. It creates a loop of over-eating to satisfy followed by the shame of knowing you just ate too much. Immediately following the need to shove your emotions down with more food to satisfy your feelings. Eating disorders are real, but they do not define you, nor should they control you. Only proceed with the 'extra now and then' if you can control it, without sabotaging your future self. By 'future self' I mean the 'you' that is going to be doing the internal monologue in thirty minutes, post-binge.

Confidence is a habit, not a trait. And it starts with how you talk to yourself. Let us start to build it. Especially when it is hard, and every time, whenever necessary.

Another way to begin building the trait of confidence is to find something you like about yourself every time you look in the mirror. Every. Day.

I must include that this includes when you use your camera phone to check your makeup or take a selfie. I challenge you to start telling yourself how pretty your eyes are, or how pretty you look when your hair falls that one certain way around your face.

Starting with small features will lead to finding bigger features about yourself more flattering. You will not only start to believe you are as pretty as your loved ones say you are, but you will start to see it, too.

I also challenge you to stop comparing yourself to other women in real life or on social media. I know Jennifer Aniston is gorgeous, but honey, so are you.

I know the girl at Walmart with the messy bun, no makeup, and baggy sweats that dangle off her small frame is effortlessly pretty, but honey, so are you.

You do not have to be her kind of pretty, remember?

Let us stop shaming ourselves when we do not feel any kind of pretty. Let us, instead, tell ourselves that we are anyways. Let us also remember the age-old tale that we say when we claim that God does not make mistakes. That includes how He made you.

Also, I challenge you to stop being the mean girl to other girls when you are feeling that extra dose of pretty. With all my respect to Miranda Lambert, let us stop projecting levels of pretty onto other women. We are not just like anyone. We are perfect the way we are.

I can guarantee that whatever shame you are projecting onto the girl in the snack aisle with unwashed hair and holey sweats, she is saying the same thing to herself. Actually, that may not be true. She may also be also be there coping post-breakup and reminding herself that she is a queen just like you. You do not know her story.

The belittling must stop. It is more of a reflection of the belittler than the *belittl-ee*. It is merely projecting your insecurity onto someone else. Stop, Regina George. Maybe not every girl wants to wear pink on Wednesdays because she would rather wear black. There is no right way to look or be, remember.

Let it no go unsaid that I like the movie *Mean Girls* as well as the song "Only Prettier". I just do not think that they are behaviors that women should project onto other women, or within themselves. Kindness always wins.

This includes kindness to ourselves.

When has it ever made you feel better to engage in self-demeaning internal monologues that have left you with mascara-stained cheeks and puffy eyes? My guess is that it never has.

For those of you who have children, consider this: when you tell your child he/she is beautiful, you know you mean it and believe it, even if, when they get older, they may not. Who is it for anyone to not believe their own mother, when she says they are beautiful? It is not bias; she believes it to be truth. Same with your best gal pals. When one of them tells you of the beauty they see in you, and you reciprocate that to them, who is anyone to say that is a lie? Sometimes, we must believe others when they tell us they think we are beautiful. Otherwise, we are calling them a liar.

Let us start receiving compliments as truth and not as words that puff us up and make us feel better when we are feeling low or less than. May we receive them as affirmations of the truth that we must start telling ourselves.

When the girls at school made fun of the girl with the not-on-trend-clothes, or a shirt that was not as flattering as they thought it should be, we learn that this kind of talk, as well as other types like it, is okay because it becomes normalized and then becomes engrained. We take it with us into adulthood, and without realizing what we are doing or saying, we inwardly—or outwardly—shame the girl who does not fit the societal standard of pretty. We also do the same thing to ourselves when we go into the fitting room or try to find an outfit we feel good in when we have not yet lost the "baby weight". Suddenly, we have a whole town of girls raising their hands, because they have been victimized by our slanderous words, like the end of *Mean Girls*. We also often fail to realize that we are included in that group. We, too, are victims of the way we speak to ourselves.

I hate the saying, "sticks and stones may break my bones, but words will never hurt me". It is a lie. Words hurt worse than sticks and stones because words leave scars on our minds, bodies and hearts for an unforeseeable amount of time, whereas scratches and scrapes on the surface heal within a week or two. Words can build up, as well as tear down. Words have power and impact. Let us choose wisely the words we speak to people, including our own self.

This also includes self-deprecating humor. You know exactly the kind I mean. The jokes we make about "if I had a thigh gap, my phone would have dropped in the toilet" or "fat people are harder to kidnap, so eat the cake". Let us not reduce our bodies to eCard puns and meme punchlines just to feel better about how much we do not like ourselves. I would rather you embrace your curves because *baby, your body is like a back road, and your man is in a hurry to take his time.* If you are single, know that a man who is worthy of your greatness and glory will also be in a hurry to take the time and learn the curves of your skin. Know that any man that is worthy of your time and treasures and talents will never make you feel like you should fit into a mold you do not belong in. Embrace your beauty for what it is: a gift from God to us all. We need you to embrace your perfect body as it is now, because there is a generation of young girls watching how we speak to ourselves and treat our bodies. There is a generation of young boys learning how to embrace their being, and they are watching. My son is skin and bones with a hollow leg. He eats us out of house and home and, yet, he is someone who thinks he thinks he is fat. God help us. Our children are watching. Our nieces, our nephews, and our neighbor's kids are watching. They are listening and taking notes to see what is acceptable and how to treat themselves. Learn how to embrace who you are for, not only yourself, but for them. Let us raise up a generation of men and women who are not looking to *GQ* or *Cosmopolitan* for the standard of nice-looking. Let them see the standard when they look in the mirror, because we modeled that for them.

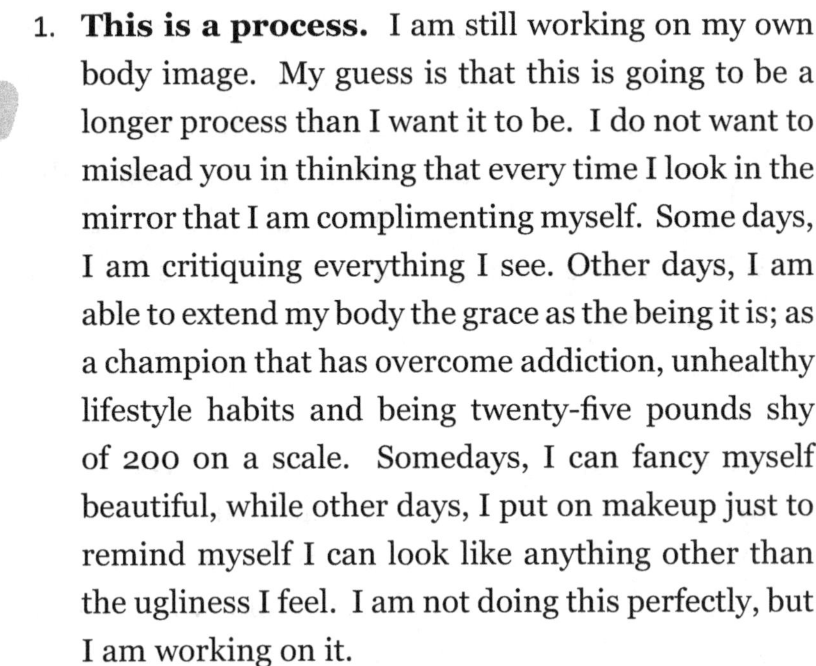

1. **This is a process.** I am still working on my own body image. My guess is that this is going to be a longer process than I want it to be. I do not want to mislead you in thinking that every time I look in the mirror that I am complimenting myself. Some days, I am critiquing everything I see. Other days, I am able to extend my body the grace as the being it is; as a champion that has overcome addiction, unhealthy lifestyle habits and being twenty-five pounds shy of 200 on a scale. Somedays, I can fancy myself beautiful, while other days, I put on makeup just to remind myself I can look like anything other than the ugliness I feel. I am not doing this perfectly, but I am working on it.

2. **I started calling my body she/her instead of "it".** This was an idea brought about when reading Jen Hatmaker's *Fierce, Free, and Full of Fire.* In it, she contributes this idea to a book she read by Hillary McBride called *Mothers, Daughters, and Body Image.* Paraphrasing both, our body is an integrated part of our whole being. Calling our body, a "she", instead of "it" reminds us that the mind and body are both equally *us*. Our character, soul, experiences, intelligence, goodness, and talents are entwined with the mind and body. She has brought us through all the things that have led us up to this day. Taking on that mentality has been the single

biggest thing to change how I speak to myself. It makes it more personal than anything else when it comes to how we speak to the self. When we take on that narrative of our bodies being a person, rather than a thing we have learned to detest and degrade, we are more apt to say nicer things, as if we are talking to a friend. It has been said, "If you wouldn't say it to your best friend, don't say it to yourself". This is gospel truth. When we speak kindly to ourselves, it drastically changes the way we feel about ourselves. Treat your body as the champion she is.

3. **Reminding myself of how far I have come in this body.** I have to remind myself that I am not the person I used to be. I have overcome some of the most horrific traumas and obstacles, and here I stand: a champion with a crown amid the falling confetti. Living in a past body is something I still do from time to time, and I have to snap myself back to present day and remember that it is still a work in progress. I often remind myself of how unhealthy it was for me to abuse my body with starvation or binge eating, punishing myself or eating laxatives like candy to "flush" out what I ate. I felt out of control with how I was mistreating and abusing my body because I did not like the way I look or felt about myself. I am now on another side of the spectrum where I eat clean(ish) and can run long distances, just because I am able and want to. I feel more in control of my body and the way she looks, based on taking control of what I could, such as what I put on my plate, or whether I talk myself out of a workout. Or be like Nike, and just do it. I have come a long way, but I still have a long way to go. It is safe to say that when we take control in

a more healthy fashion of the things we have dominion over in our lives, we are on the right track to love ourselves more efficiently and more courageously than we ever have before.

Whatever season you are in in life, it is never too late to rewrite your story. It is never too late to take charge of your narrative and choose to live a better, more fulfilled life. It is not too late to start living the story you want to tell. It is not too late to start showing up a as a different person than you once were. I am here to tell you that no matter where you have come from, or what you have been through, there is purpose in the pain and a message within your mess. I remember laying on the cold bathroom floor after having overdosed. I had awoken from a blackout and saw the death in my eyes, and I heard the voice of God say, "This is not the life I have for you." If I was to start living a different life, I knew I had to choose to make change. Jesus can only help you if you choose to use your God-given free will and help yourself make change. Certainly, He will be there for you when you call on Him to help you, but YOU must choose to exercise your right to start living the life you want to live. I am convinced that you were made for a life that is more than what it has become. I am convinced that your darkest chapter has a bright light at the end of the tunnel to be used as a guide for other people to know there is hope. I am convinced that you were put on this planet to be more and do more. I am certain that you can bounce back from whatever rock-bottom you may find yourself in. I know that you can crawl your way out of the pit, because I have done it time and time again. I am here as a living proof that Jesus is real, and that God can turn any mess into a message and that one day, your story will be someone else's navigation to finding their way back to the life they had, or to the one they want to live. I know your struggle is real, and I know that it is hard. I know that at times it sucks, and we want to throw in the towel, but let us remember that throwing in the towel only adds to laundry, and if anything sucks more in life, it is folding laundry.

I also know that your struggle is not uncommon. I know you know that, too. I know you know that you are not the only one facing the dragons you are slaying. I know you know that there is more for you out in this world than the life you have settled for. I know that your heart is ready and willing for something more. I know that you are scared, and it may be lonely to face this battle you may not be ready to fight. I also know that if you wait until you are ready, you will never get there. No one is ever ready to do something hard and challenging they have never done before, without any kind of experience or training. I was never ready to leave behind norms I was comfortable in for the chance of something better, when I did not know any different. That is why there is a first time for everything. We rarely wake up motivated to take on the challenges we face when we live in a state of uncertainty. We rarely know where to start or even how to navigate the path of the road less traveled. Sometimes, we must simply just start. Sometimes, we must be the compass that shows others the way. We must stop playing the victim—it never works out well for the victim in any story. We must stop being the villain. Only Angelina Jolie plays well, the role of Maleficent. Not everyone and everything is out to get us or working against us. Life is simply unfair to all people at times. Some more than others. Even when it seems most unfair, remind yourself of Rosa Parks, who incited the Montgomery Bus Boycott by refusing to give up her seat to a white man. She would have regretted not saying anything. Now, she is revered as one of the most influential leaders of the Civil Rights Movement. Stand up for your right to have a fair shot at what you know you deserve. Learning to be the hero of your own story is why God gives us hardships. We must learn to be the hero, so we can learn how to guide others out of their own messes and trials.

It has been said that when life gives you lemons, make lemonade. We would not have such anthems as "Formation" or "Freedom", had Beyoncé not called on women to take back control of the narrative and the goodness that is deserved. Do not let the hand life has dealt you in a hard season be the thing that breaks you. Persevere through the hard. Embrace the suck. Prove them all wrong.

Show them you were made for this.

Acknowledgments

Thank you, Jesus. You have personally taken the mess that was my life and turned it into a message for the world to marvel. Your glory, mercy, forgiveness, and grace will forever be at the top of my most cherished list. Without you, I am nothing, can do nothing, and am nothing. Praise You.

Thank you, to my husband. You not only encouraged me to write this book, you also continue to be my personal cheerleader and encourager. You are a mirror I can look into and see all the beauty within me, and the things I need to work on to be a better woman, wife, Christian, mother, sister, and friend. You are the answer to my unanswered prayers from my younger days, and the answer to the pleas to the heavens for someone who made all of the wait worth it. I love you.

To my son. You have no idea how much I marvel at your being. Your hugs are healing, and your smile makes my heart soar. You have always been the greatest reason I have to stay sober, to continue working towards health, and to continue working on being the best me that I can be, for you. I love you 'mostest'.

To my parents, who never stopped believing in me, and always gave me the love every child longs for. Dad, you always told me that I can do anything I set my mind to. Now look! I wrote a book! Mom, you have been the one constant champion in my life. Always fighting even when it hurt, and it was hard. I admire you more than you will ever know.

To my tribe: Christine, Eve, Nina, Natascha, and Kaylee. You have shown me true friendship. You have shown me what it is genuinely like to belong. You ladies inspire me, motivate me, and are the epitome of a girl gang. I love you and am so grateful for you and the friendships we have.

To my home church family at *Agape*. I hope I am making you all proud. I hope you see the fruits of your labor you graciously and lovingly bestowed upon me. I miss and love you all more than words can articulate. Thank you for always being my home away from home.

To Tonya. Thank you for your unending friendship and your words of encouragement and wisdom in my life. You have always been a safe place for me to land. I am forever grateful.

To my church family in the Poconos. Matt and Sol. Kenny and Amanda. Dave and Bekah. Tara, Denise, Joann, and Yvonne. You have all breathed life and love into me, and I am grateful to know you, and worship among you.

To me, myself, and I. This may seem vain, but I must acknowledge the labor of love that is this book. We powered through tough and triggering chapters. Typed with tears streaming down our face and gave this body chills when the words came out just right. I must give myself some credit for being able to accomplish a dream I have had for years. In my most ecstatic Elle Woods voice at the Harvard graduation, "WE DID IT!"

References

Chapter One: 1. Joshua 1:5

Chapter Two: 1. James 1:2&3

                2. Ephesians 4:32

                3. Matthew 18:21&22

Chapter Four: 1. Basic Human Needs by Tony Robbins

Habitsforwellbeing.com/6-core-human-needs-by-   anthony-robbins

                2. AZQuotes.com

                3. John 8:7-11

Chapter Five: 1. John 8:36

                2. Matthew 6:24

                3. John 19:1

                4. Tony Robbins

Chapter Seven: 1. Matthew 26:41, Mark 14:38

Chapter Eight: Hebrews 10:10

Chapter 11:   John 5:1-18

Chapter 12:   1. 2 Corinthians 6:14

                2. Ephesians 5:1

                3. Romans 3:23

                4. Hebrews 10:26

                Fierce, Free, and Full of Fire, Jen Hatmaker, pg. 45,46

                5. Romans 8:1

                6. Matthew 4:1-17

                7. Proverbs 28:13

Conclusion: Psalm 139:14